British Hard Plastic Dolls 1946–1960

INCLUDING COMPOSITION AND VINYL

Makers: Rosebud, Roddy, Pedigree
Doll names: **Rosebud Knee Joint Girl,
Roddy Top Knot Baby, Pedigree
Negro Baby**
Sizes: 17"/43cm, 8"/20cm, 16"/40.5cm
Marks: 'Rosebud Made in Eng'; 'Roddy
Made in Eng'; 'Pedigree Made in England'
Dates: 1955, 1955, 1953

Three chocolate and black-coloured hard
plastic dolls in original clothes which are
now quite hard to find in good condition.

British Hard Plastic Dolls
1946–1960

INCLUDING COMPOSITION AND VINYL

Frances Baird

New Cavendish Books
London

FRONT COVER
Makers: Pedigree, Palitoy, Pedigree
Doll names: **Pedigree Bonnie Charlie**,
Palitoy Girl Dress Me Doll, **Pedigree
Negro baby**
Sizes: 14"/35.5cm, 15"/38cm, 14"/35.5cm
Marks: 'Pedigree, Made in Eng'; 'Palitoy,
Made in Eng'; 'Pedigree, Made in England'
Dates: 1955, 1955, 1953

Three hard plastic dolls in original clothes
which are now quite hard to find in good
condition. In 1959 Bonnie Charlie was
updated and also wore a black jacket and
hat. (Photograph by Mark Williams)

First edition published in Great Britain
by New Cavendish Books

Designed by Jacky Wedgwood

Photography by Mark Williams and
Colin WDP Greene

Edited by Narisa Chakra

Typesetting by Dorchester Typesetting
Group Limited, Dorset

Printed by Bangkok Printing (1984) Co., Ltd.

ISBN 1 872727 41 7

ACKNOWLEDGEMENTS
Special thanks to Christine Wimsey,
who shares with me the same interest
and dedication in this era of dolls and
for her help and enthusiasm
throughout. Also to Peter, Simon and
Julian Baird, Bob Brechin, Alice
Brooker, Richard Lines, Ray
G. Mitchell, Rosemary Palmer, the late
Bill Pugh, Jane Raybould, Lesley and
Dave Simpson, Denise and Tony Slade,
Ann Strudwick, Joan and Robin Toone,
Margaret and Jack Treweek, Brian
Turner, Peggy and Roy Woollett, for
their friendship, interest and valuable
help.

All the dolls illustrated are from the
author's collection unless otherwise
stated.

Contents

Foreword

Group of British hard plastic dolls
Back row, left to right:
Roddy 22"/56cm black **HA Walkie Talkie** 1955
Sarold 25"/64cm bent leg **Toddler** 1950
BND 21"/53.5cm **HA Walkie Talkie** 1952
Middle row, left to right:
Palitoy 18"/46cm Petal Skin **Toddler** 1957
W. & ST. 12"/30.5cm **Walkie** 1953
Pedigree 20"/51cm black **Toddler** 1952
Front row, left to right:
Rosebud 13"/33cm bent leg **Toddler** 1952
Rosebud 11"/28cm bent leg baby 1955

Having been interested in dolls for over forty years, it is wonderful to be able to share my experience and knowledge of hard plastic dolls with other collectors by writing and illustrating a doll history covering this beautiful but short era.

Many people at doll fairs have asked me how I can tell one doll from another at a glance. The answer has to be my years of experience in handling hard plastic dolls, plus a lifetime's interest in them. I have also gleaned a few tips over the years which I'll gladly pass on in the following pages. My interest in dolls goes back as far as I can remember, probably to when I was given my first doll. Hours of my childhood were spent dressing and playing with these dolls in the late 1940s and early 1950s, although as a small child I did not so much 'collect' dolls as hope for a doll as a birthday or Christmas present. My collecting started seriously when I was working and saw a beautiful, large, modern doll hanging on the front of a dust-cart, obviously thrown out by an unenthusiastic youngster and used on the cart as a 'mascot'. I compared this beautiful doll with the plainer, moulded-hair, composition dolls available in our local town during the early 1940s, and decided it was too attractive to be thrown away. As a result, I began to rescue other interesting dolls and to collect a few new ones too. I was hooked!

Over the decades my collection has grown considerably and having photographed the dolls, my task then was to correctly identify them and re-dress the ones that had lost their clothes in as suitable and near-original outfits as possible.

During my research I came across many helpful people only too pleased to tell of the dolls they once owned and some that were sadly broken. It is never too late to start a collection and dolls are a rewarding and attractive hobby. This era of dolls includes most of the well-known British manufacturers of hard plastic dolls who marketed children's play dolls between 1946 and 1964. Regrettably many of them are no longer in business, but their lovely dolls are remembered in this book.

Introduction

Hard plastic dolls were made for a short period after the Second World War from a material based on cellulose acetate which was perfected during the war for use on aircraft parts. Many of the British doll factories were requisitioned for the 'war effort' and it was therefore a natural progression to turn this new material to their own use once the hostilities had ceased and the factories reverted to their previous business of doll and toy making.

The most prolific doll-makers in Britain at the end of the Second World War were companies such as British National Dolls, Palitoy, Pedigree, Roddy and Rosebud, with perhaps Pedigree being the major producer of hard plastic dolls and Palitoy experimenting with early vinyl type dolls. Since the demise of almost all of these names, post-war dolls have become a popular field, with collectors thirsting for more knowledge of these beautiful and durable hard plastic dolls. Many of these pre-war firms had started in the business of doll making with bisque, celluloid or composition, and switched production to injection-moulded cellulose acetate in 1946. Hard plastic dolls were to enjoy at least ten glorious years before another new material, 'vinyl', superceded them in the mid- to late-Fifties.

Many companies tried different combinations of plastics to achieve the desired effect, advertising their dolls as the 'best quality', the 'most beautiful', the 'most realistic' and 'all English made in our own factory' (just as they had advertised composition dolls a decade before!). They claimed the dolls made from the new material were indestructible, not shattering like bisque or celluloid, and not crazing or powdering like composition. However, in their rush to compete with each other, companies often used combinations of doll parts and existing moulds from their pre-war days so that early examples resembled the composition dolls. They would also purchase doll parts from one another and share moulds in their efforts to complete large orders, which explains why one can sometimes find oddities or two identical dolls with different makers' marks.

Most companies of the day marked their dolls on the back of the neck or body, or both. However, as many dolls were made for department and chain stores as special orders, they were not marked on their backs, but on the box only, or were perhaps even given the store's own brand name, or just a 'dolly' name. Therefore dolls can often be found with no marks at all, or with simply 'Made in England' on their backs. However, with experience, they are still easily recognisable as being from a particular maker.

A group of composition dolls made in the 1930s and 1940s. Hard plastics followed these by the late '40s and, where factories were still using old moulds, many early ones resembled the composition doll faces.

A group of unmarked dolls probably made to special order for department and chain stores and marked only on their boxes. The dolls are of course recognisable by their faces and body construction. All are hard plastics.

The method of manufacturing these dolls varied from one company to another in as much as they all had their own 'secret' recipe which was jealously guarded and which, in many instances, has now been destroyed. The basic process though was similar and consisted of the molten plastic substance being poured into original design moulds (these moulds having first been designed by a sculptor or doll artist and cast in two halves in metal, usually aluminium). The molten plastic was then left to solidify under heat for the necessary length of time required to achieve the desired thickness. The surplus was poured off, leaving a gelled layer on the metal mould which was reheated to 'cure' the plastic. After curing, the mould was water-cooled, opened up and the moulding removed. The hollow bodies or parts were then trimmed and cleaned ready for sealing the half limbs together lengthwise with any hooks or attachments affixed. They were then ready for dipping in colour and painting as necessary. Lastly, eyes were inserted, wigs adhered and parts strung or pushed together, depending upon the type of doll being made. As the factories became more mechanised, these procedures were adapted to the new machinery, and the injection-moulding era had begun. Dolls could be turned out faster than ever before, keeping abreast of demand more quickly and efficiently. In addition, they were more lightweight and inexpensive.

These new hard plastic dolls were eagerly bought by parents whose young children had had few or no toys to play with during the war years, and by parents wanting the best for their post-war 'boom' babies growing up in the late Forties and early Fifties. As one of the 'army' of post-war babies, the author well remembers the doll displays in toy shops, department and chain stores of 1950. The hard plastic dolls themselves had a pleasing, hard, smooth, shiny appearance which cannot be dented with the fingernails and is distinguishable from hard vinyl which does mark under pressure of this sort. The hard plastic heads were moulded in two halves and joined together lengthwise, having a seam down each side just behind the ears. Later vinyl heads did not have this seam as they were moulded in one piece, with the hair usually rooted into the vinyl. Hard plastic dolls were made with either moulded hair, or a glued-on mohair wig or soft saran nylon wig in later models. They had sleeping and/or flirting eyes, and five joints – head, arms and legs – that moved. The dolls were lighter in weight and easier to handle than their heavy composition predecessors. Most had 'ma-ma' voice boxes and many had hand-assisted walking mechanisms, while a few had 'knee-joints', enabling the doll to sit or kneel naturally and realistically.

Doll dressing was a popular pastime among mothers and grandmothers during the Forties and Fifties and many dolls were sold naked from shop counter displays for their new owners to dress.

BELOW LEFT
Knee joint dolls which sit and kneel very realistically. These two are 1955 Pedigree but they were also made by Palitoy, Roddy and Rosebud in varying sizes and are very sought after by collectors today.

BELOW RIGHT
Dolly dressmaking and knitting sets were very popular in the 1940s and 1950s and most little girls would have found one in their Christmas stockings. They usually contained fabrics, sewing thread, paper patterns, scissors, needle and thimble – in fact everything to dress one's favourite dolls. The knitting sets contained small balls of wool in a pretty range of colours, knitting needles, directions on how to knit and sometimes a plastic wool holder.

One of the black negro-type dolls made in the early 1950s when many immigrant families came to Britain in search of work. The one illustrated is a 10"/25.5cm bent leg baby and marked Pedigree. These dolls were sold wearing gingham or striped dresses/rompers.

An unmarked baby from around 1950. Probably attributable to one of the many doll-makers of the period that only stayed in business for a few years. With records now destroyed he is virtually unidentifiable. (Collection Christine Wimsey)

Patterns for dolls' clothes were regularly featured in women's magazines of the day and doll dressmaking and knitting sets were available for little girls to dress their own dolls and learn new skills. Boxed dolls were costumed in cotton, taffeta, voile, organdie, lace, net, seersucker, sailcloth, velvet or gingham, whichever was most easily accessible following the war years. Some were even clothed in plastic dresses and bonnets, all of which soon disintegrated with constant play, dressing and washing, making an early doll found in its original outfit a much-sought-after acquisition among collectors today. The dolls of this era were dressed in the style of little girls, boys and babies. Popular outfits were party dresses, school uniforms, ballet dresses, wedding gowns, fairy costumes and brownie uniforms.

Families of dolls were made from the same head mould and companies would make the most of a popular face, using it to make many sizes of the same doll with several different hair styles and colours, or without a wig for dressing as a boy. Body styles could have straight or bent legs, and the plastic could be coloured flesh pink or black, allowing dozens of variations from the same mould.

In the late Forties, due to a labour shortage, black immigrant families from the West Indies were recruited to live and work in Britain, filling jobs in hospitals, factories and on public transport. Doll companies were quick to increase production of their range of black plastic dolls to fulfil the new demand. They also made special moulds for such dolls with moulded tight curls or astrakhan wigs. These dolls became very popular in the early Fifties, but are more difficult to find today.

Although many companies started in a small way in the late Forties with just a dozen employees, their directors visited the United States looking for the latest machinery and techniques, and returned with large orders and machinery capable of making many thousands of dolls a day. These companies soon grew to quadruple the size of their workforce and their order books by the late Fifties, when the hey-day of the British doll industry began.

It has been extremely difficult to research the actual quantities of individual hard plastic dolls made, many companies stating that the old records had been destroyed and some not wanting to divulge that information. Suffice it to say, these dolls were mass produced. Many thousands would be made of the popular lines, with fewer being produced if the doll was withdrawn after only a year. There were also many small companies starting up around 1950 which only stayed in business for a few years. Many of these dolls were largely unmarked and are now almost impossible to trace.

Dating an old doll can be difficult and is rarely ever truly accurate. Catalogues do help if the doll is still in its original clothes, as it can be identified to a particular year. However, if the doll has lost its original outfit it can only be dated to the period of a production run, which can be as long as six years with a popular line. On average a doll was marketed for about three years, and six out of every ten dolls were usually blondes, as it was thought the majority of little girls would choose a blonde.

'Dolls' hospitals' in every town during the Fifties could provide repair work on hard plastic dolls by replacing broken limbs, heads, eyes and wigs to make a doll look new again. As the dolls were moulded in two halves, and seamed together lengthwise, they would often split open when dropped, either on the body or down one limb. The wigs too did not withstand too rough a treatment, but could easily be replaced. Companies such as Chad Valley made a lovely range of replacement wigs in fair or brunette colours for these dolls throughout the Forties and Fifties, which were available through dolls' hospitals or by post from magazine advertisements. A few of my own dolls were re-wigged in this way, and I would choose either short curly, or the two long plaits style and give my favourite dolls a change of hairstyle.

Chad Valley and Lines Bros Tri-ang Toys made many accessories for little girls to play with, including tea sets for dolls' tea parties, saucepan sets, pastry sets and cutlery sets all in silver aluminium, or sometimes the tea sets were painted in pastel colours, and boxed in plain brown cardboard cartons with an attractive picture on the lid.

Advertisements like this one appeared in many magazines and children's comics throughout the 1940s and 1950s, offering a lovely range of replacement wigs to renew or update your favourite doll.

A Chad Valley cooking set from the late 1940s, which included a saucepan with lid, frying pan, milk pan, preserve pan, collander, mixing bowl, measuring cup and bun tin. Lines Bros Tri-ang Toys made similar sets.

This Chad Valley pastry set from the 1960s includes scales, mixing bowl with spoon, rolling pin and board, dummy ingredients, patty tins and recipe leaflet.

A Chad Valley kiddies' cutlery box from the 1950s. A little wooden tray containing four each of knives, forks and spoons. Just the thing for a little girl's Christmas stocking.

Many types of modern dolls were made during this era and can be divided roughly into five groups: baby dolls, toddler dolls, girl/boy dolls, fashion and costume dolls and dolls' house dolls. Most companies made dolls from each group and the collector can start by choosing one particular group, by collecting a mixture from all groups, from one or two favourite companies, or even a favourite size. Baby dolls are probably the most widely available of all doll types as most little girls were given one of these as their very first doll. They usually had moulded hair, a realistic baby-type face, clenched fists and the familiar bent limbs denoting a baby doll. Many were sold dressed only in a nappy, but, of course, boxed dolls wore attractive party dresses or christening gowns and bonnets. Toddler dolls were the 'older' babies, also with bent limbs, but with more detailed hands and an older child-like face with wide eyes, expressive mouths, usually with a tongue and teeth, and a curly wig. Whereas girl dolls had straight legs, often walking-talking mechanisms, longer hairstyles and older, attractive faces, the moulded hair versions could be dressed as boys. Teenage or 'fashion dolls' as they were called in the Forties and early Fifties, had straight legs and slimmer bodies and were usually provided with paper patterns to make extra fashion clothes for them. Very few teenage dolls with uplifted busts and painted-on make-up as we know them today were made in hard plastic. Costume dolls were small, usually six or seven inches tall, and were dressed in colourful outfits from around the world, as well as storybook characters and the professions such as nurse, policeman, soldier, sailor etc. Fairy dolls and ballerinas were also made in this size.

The quantity and variety of dolls that have survived from this decade of hard plastic dolls are extremely diverse, with perhaps their only common denominator being the fact that they were all made and produced in England.

For the convenience of the readers, I have arranged the hard plastic dolls into chapters dealing with their respective manufacturers arranged in alphabetical order. Only costume dolls which form a separate genre of collecting are grouped together into the significant manufacturers of such dolls. I hope this book will shed new light on a fascinating collecting subject.

Airfix Industries Ltd

1939 TO THE PRESENT DAY

Not normally associated with doll-making, this company was founded as a family business by the Kove family in London in 1939 and called Airfix Products Ltd. They manufactured air-filled rubber toys and injection-moulded plastic rattles and combs during the war years, and were probably one of the largest manufacturers of these items in the mid-Forties. By 1948 they were producing small plastic dolls, including fairy dolls for Christmas decorations. **Anne** was a named, 3" plastic doll of 1948, with jointed limbs, as were other small plastic dolls registered in 1955 as 'Amanda' dolls. However, probably their most popular and now most easily found doll was the 5" **Fairy**. This little doll had a one-piece, glossy, hard plastic head and body with jointed swinging arms, moulded hair and painted features. The arms were able to swing very easily as they were slotted into place before the two body parts were sealed together lengthwise. These small plastic dolls were sold from counter displays in stores throughout Britain in the Fifties, either dressed as a fairy (of which 1000s were sold at Christmas), or naked to be dressed at home. They also worked well as

Maker: Airfix
Doll name: none
Size: 5"/12.5cm
Marks: 'Airfix Made in England' across shoulders
Date: late 1940s

These three dolls could be purchased from shop counter displays naked and then dressed for a dolls house. They had fixed bodies with movable arms only, but could be stood or laid on the beds and were inexpensive and popular as they could be dressed as male or female.

Maker: Airfix
Doll name: none
Size: 5"/12.5cm
Marks: 'Airfix Made in England' across shoulders
Date: late 1940s

The hard plastic shiny body with swinging arms can be seen clearly. Also note the painted features, moulded hair and shoes.

Maker: Airfix
Doll name: none
Size: 5"/12.5cm
Marks: 'Airfix Made in England' across shoulders
Date: late 1940s and early 1950s

This illustration shows the maker's mark across the shoulders. All Airfix small shiny hard plastic dolls were marked in this way. The many imitations were not marked.

This drawing shows how the arms are secured as the two moulded halves are joined together, on these Airfix 5"/12.5cm hard plastic dolls.

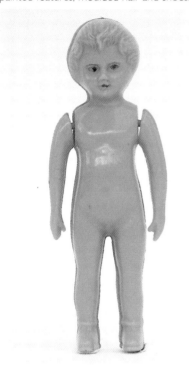  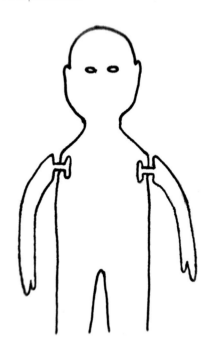

dolls' house dolls as they had a universal hairstyle that looked delightful dressed as either a girl or boy. All the small plastic dolls were marked 'Airfix Made in England' across their backs, thus making them easily identifiable from a range of foreign copies on sale during those years.

The Airfix doll range, however, was quite small, as they were more famous for their enormously popular plastic construction kits introduced from 1954 to the present day. In 1957 the company went public and changed the name to Airfix Industries, and in 1962 expanded, taking over Semco Dolls Ltd, who at that time were producing a range of large vinyl dolls. Airfix ceased manufacture of the Semco doll range, but continued to make a few vinyl dolls periodically through the Seventies, with **Summertime Girls, Walking Baby Loves You, Sweet Dreams** and a **Farrah Fawcett** teen-type doll, to name but a few of their vinyl doll range.

◀ PAGE 14
Maker: Airfix Industries Ltd
Doll name: **Fairy** (centre doll)
Size: 5"/12.5cm
Marks: 'Airfix Made in England'
Dates: late 1940s/early 1950s

Three typical small Airfix dolls showing one dressed for the Coronation, one fairy in crêpe paper, net and tinsel and one nude for dressing at home.

Amanda Jane Ltd

1952 TO THE PRESENT DAY

This company began in 1952 by making dolls' clothes and accessories in nine sizes and registered as 'Amanda Jane' after the two daughters of the proprietors Commander Conrad and Mrs Elsin Rawnsley. Their Fifties-style hats, shoes and dresses were sold in many leading London stores, as they were then a London-based company operating from the Commander's flat following his retirement from the Royal Navy. Such names as 'Budget Collection', priced from around two shillings and 'Model Collection', priced from about five shillings, were to be seen in their booklets which pictured lovely named dresses, skirts, blouses, cardigans, sunsuits, beachwear, school/nurse/riding/brownie/bridal outfits, coats and hats, as well as footwear in a range of sizes to suit dolls from 7" to 20". In addition, there were many accessories and jewellery for the well-dressed doll, and even furniture.

The company moved to Sussex in 1957, and their first doll, an 8" hard plastic little girl with a glued-on mohair wig, tiny sleeping eyes without lashes and fully jointed elastic strung limbs was introduced in 1958. This lovely little girl doll was called **Jinx** and bore a passing resemblance to **Miss Rosebud**, but was marked only 'England' across her back. **Jinx** was available with a blonde, auburn or brunette wig, had attractive rosy cheeks and was the only hard plastic doll introduced by the company. Her very own collection of fashion clothes was produced in separate packs, as **Jinx** could be purchased naked ready for dressing in a cellophane bag, tagged with a card which stated 'Jinx by Amanda Jane – Buy me and collect my wonderful trousseau'. She was priced at four shillings and sixpence. Her outfits, the 'Jinx

◀ PAGE 16
Maker: Amanda Jane Ltd
Doll name: **Jinx**
Size: 8"/20cm
Marks: 'England'
Date: 1958

A blonde and brunette **Jinx** in original clothes. Many attractive outfits were available for these little hard plastic dolls.

Maker: Amanda Jane
Doll name: **Jinx**
Size: 8"/20cm
Marks: 'England' across back
Date: 1958

This photograph shows clearly the jointed head and limbs, glued-on wig and rosy cheeks. These dolls had sleeping eyes with no lashes and were available in fair, auburn or brunette.

Two original Amanda Jane dresses from the 1950s. The dress on the right was called 'Banjo'. They came in assorted sizes and each little dress has the Amanda Jane label sewn into the side seam.

Colour Package Sets' and 'Jinx Budget Sets', were similar to the original range of Amanda Jane clothes and were priced from around one shilling to ten shillings with attractive names such as 'Juanita', 'Biarritz', 'Grisette', 'Piazza' and many more. Each tiny Amanda Jane outfit had the Amanda Jane label stitched into it, making them easily recognisable today. Accessories and furniture were also available for **Jinx**.

In the early Sixties the company switched to vinyl, introducing two girl dolls, both 12" tall, this time called **Amanda** and **Jane**, and a 14" baby called **Bubbles**. The little hard plastic **Jinx** and the larger sizes of dolls' clothing and accessories were discontinued.

In 1963 the company changed hands and began to produce just one small vinyl girl doll called **Amanda Jane**. She was 7" tall with larger sleeping eyes and eyelashes, entirely in hard vinyl with rooted, short hair, available in three colours.

In 1977 (Royal Silver Jubilee Year), the company celebrated 25 years in business. They have continued to make beautiful outfits for their range of small vinyl dolls to the present day, updating them periodically to keep abreast of the times, and introducing babies and black dolls to their range for the Eighties.

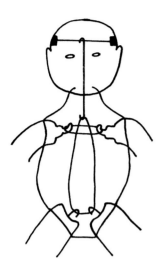

This rough sketch shows how **Jinx** is strung. The legs have wire hooks and the arms moulded plastic ones. The head is strung through to the legs and the arms are strung separately.

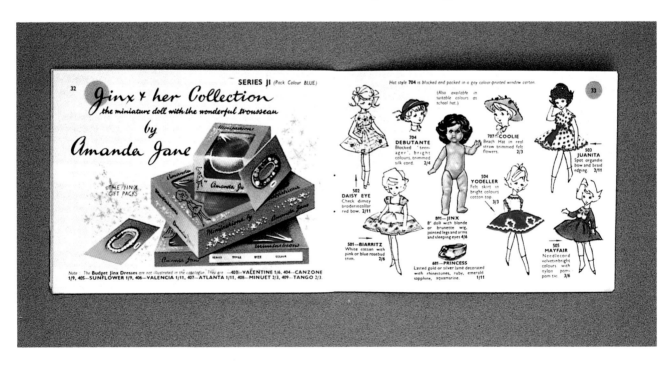

Taken from the Amanda Jane 1960 collection, this illustration shows some of the fashions that were available for **Jinx**, plus the doll herself, priced at four shillings and sixpence.

Maker: Amanda Jane
Doll name: **Jinx**
Size: 8"/20cm
Marks: 'England' across back
Date: 1958

Jinx as she was sold in her cellophane wrapper with a card tag stating 'Jinx by Amanda Jane – buy me and collect my wonderful trousseau'.

This illustration shows some of the colour coded, boxed **Jinx** outfits together with an Amanda Jane catalogue.

Maker: Crolly Ireland
Doll name: **Amanda Jane**
Size: 11"/28cm
Marks: 'Crolly Made in Ireland'
Date: early 1960s

This series of dolls were vinyl with rooted nylon hair in blonde or brunette and dressed in a variety of outfits made by the Amanda Jane company.
(Collection Denise and Tony Slade)

Maker: Amanda Jane
Doll name: **Jinx**
Size: 8"/20cm
Marks: 'England' across back
Date: 1958

The brunette and auburn Jinx model two sundresses. On the left, white with red trim and on the right, green with white trim.

Brunette Jinx on the left, models 'Scottish Girl' in red tartan with black bolero and beret. Jinx on the right models raincoat and hat in turquoise and white check.

Brunette Jinx on the left models pink check baby doll nightie, and auburn-haired Jinx on the right models pale pink nightie and pink trimmed white dressing gown.

British National Dolls

North London based, this company started in the 1930s making china-headed girl dolls with composition bodies and glued-on mohair wigs or moulded-head babies. They commenced manufacturing all-composition dolls with lovely pearly teeth and glued-on mohair wigs in the early 1940s, and one of their early named dolls was **Sunshine Babs**. They were said to be the first company to mass produce the all-composition baby/girl/boy dolls in a large range of sizes, and by the late Forties registered the name Skintex for their dolls.

During the early 1950s this company switched to making a wide range of hard plastic dolls, including babies, toddlers and girls in various sizes using some of the same composition face moulds, with and without voice boxes. Walking-talking girl dolls with sleeping eyes, open closed mouths with a tongue and lovely mohair wigs in several colours, sizes and styles, including the popular two long plaits style were made in the Fifties. These 21" hand-assisted walking-talking dolls had a stomach grille and ma-ma voice box and were called 'Dollie Walkers'. They came with the following instructions on how to walk and sit your new doll:

Maker: BND
Doll name: **Skintex**
Sizes: baby 12"/30.5cm, girl 18"/46cm
Marks: both dolls marked 'BND London' on their backs
Date: early 1940s

The composition baby on the left has painted features, moulded hair and jointed limbs. The little girl on the right has a real hair wig which is not the original, sleeping eyes, jointed limbs and straight legs. Both are quite heavy compared to hard plastic.

Maker: BND
Doll name: **Babykins**
Size: 10"/25.5cm
Marks: 'BND London' on their backs
Date: early 1950s

These hard plastic babies were purchased from Marks & Spencer stores in the early 1950s and have been well played with, having lost some of their eyelashes. The babies have sleeping eyes, moulded hair and jointed head and limbs. They have been dressed as a pair but in actual fact are from different batches as they are different shades of pink.

Maker: BND (British National Dolls Ltd)
Doll names: **Skintex** (girl), **Babykins** (baby)
Sizes: boy 13"/33cm, girl 18"/46cm, baby 10"/25.5cm
Marks: 'BND LONDON'
Date: boy early 50s, girl early 40s, baby early 50s

This company made many china-headed and composition dolls throughout the 1930s and 1940s, moving into hard plastic for a few years before closing down.

HOW YOU WALK WITH DOLLIE WALKER ... IMPORTANT: Dollie's head should not be inclined forward as this retards the walking movement.

To walk alongside Dollie Walker, hold her by her left or right hand. Balance Dollie Walker first on one foot, then the other – just as you walk yourself. Repeat this motion as you walk.

To walk behind Dollie Walker, place your hands on her shoulders and in a walking motion, balance Dollie Walker first on one foot, then the other – and she'll walk along in front of you just like a real pal. TAKE A LITTLE WALK WITH DOLLIE WALKER.

HOW TO MAKE DOLLIE WALKER SIT ...
Dollie Walker is very obedient. Make her sit by simply pushing her legs into a sitting position one at a time. You can actually hear the legs snap into position.

DOLLY WALKER'S LUSTROUS HAIR
Comb it – Wave it – Curl it

BRITISH NATIONAL DOLLS LIMITED
LONDON – ENGLAND.

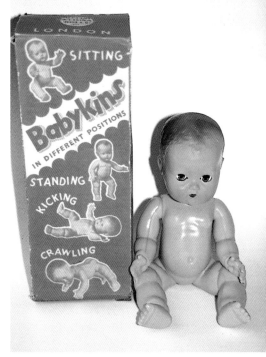

Maker: BND London
Doll name: **Babykins**
Size: 10"/25.5cm
Marks: BND London
Date: early 1950s

An undressed Babykins shown next to her original box which states: sitting, standing, kicking, crawling doll.
(Collection Denise and Tony Slade)

Maker: BND
Doll name: none
Size: 13"/33cm
Marks: 'BND London' across the back
Date: early 1950s

A toddler girl (left) and boy (right) with mohair glued-on plaited wig, sleeping eyes, ma-ma voice box with grille in the back and jointed limbs. Both have the same face and have been redressed. A toddler boy with moulded hair, sleeping eyes, ma-ma voice box with grille in his back and jointed limbs. This boy has the same face as his sister and composition girl. No original clothes; he has been redressed.

Maker: BND
Doll name: **Dollie Walker**
Size: 21"/53.5cm
Marks: 'BND London' on back
Date: 1952

The brunette-wigged version of this walking-talking doll with sleeping eyes, open closed mouth with tongue, ma-ma voice box with grille in her stomach. The hands are the large type with the seam across the palm. She wears a replica 1950s dress.

Maker: BND
Doll name: **Dollie Walker**
Size: 21"/53.5cm
Marks: 'BND London' across back
Date: early 1950s

A blonde-wigged version of the walking-talking doll, which has had her long plaits trimmed. Blue sleeping eyes, open closed mouth with tongue, ma-ma voice box with grille in her stomach and large type hands with the seam across the palms. She wears a replica of her original dress.

Maker: BND
Doll name: **Dollie Walker**
Size: 21"/53.5cm
Marks: 'BND London' on back
Date: early 1950s

This blonde walking-talking doll shown standing next to her box which states 'Dollie Walker – Does everything'. 'Did you ever see a dream walking – It's a wonderful toy'.
(Collection Christine Wimsey)

Had the instructions supplied with the dolls been heeded by the child, there would not have been so many broken dolls!

All British National Dolls were marked 'BND LONDON' on the back of their necks and the back of their bodies, and are easy to recognise by these marks. Their dresses were of cotton prints, lace and button trimmed, and the dolls were readily available from most Marks & Spencer stores and other toy stores in all large towns throughout Britain. One of the company's major buyers during the Fifties was Marks & Spencer.

By the late Fifties the company changed to rooted hair, vinyl heads on hard plastic bodies before closing down at the start of the next decade.

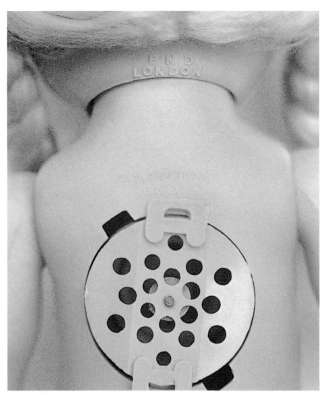

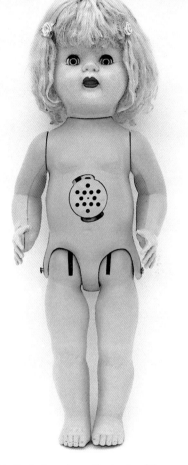

Maker: BND
Doll name: unknown
Size: 13"/33cm
Marks: 'BND London' on back of neck
Date: early 1950s

The marks on the neck of the BND toddler are easily distinguishable in this illustration. All the BND dolls are marked in this way and are easy to identify. Also shows the voice box grille in the back.

This illustration shows the body of the walking-talking doll with her ma-ma voice box and grille in the stomach.

Maker: BND
Doll name: unknown
Size: 13"/33cm
Marks: 'BND London' across the back
Date: early 1950s

This illustration shows the tubby toddler body on these toddlers. They are elastic strung and have a pleasing smooth finish.

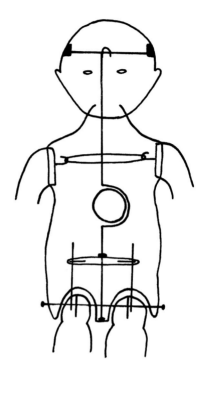

Diagram showing how the BND **Dollie Walker** is strung. She has a conventional walking mechanism with the bolt heads protruding from the plastic at the hip and the arms strung separately. The circle in the centre is the ma-ma voice box in cylindrical diaphragm form.

Maker: BND
Doll name: none
Size: 15"/38cm
Marks: 'BND London' on back
Date: late 1950s

One of the last dolls made by this company. She has the same type of smooth hard plastic body as the toddlers, but vinyl rooted hair in a short curly style, and sleeping dark blue eyes. Her head looks rather large for her body. She has a ma-ma voice box with the grille in her back.

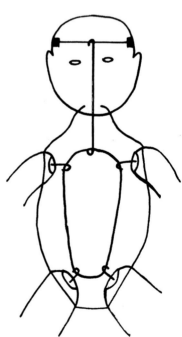

BELOW LEFT
Diagram showing the BND toddler. The legs and arms are strung together with elastic and metal hooks and the head linked in separately.

Chiltern/ H.G. Stone & Co. Ltd

DOLLS FROM 1958 TO 1967

H.G. Stone & Co. were a subsidiary company of L. Rees & Co. Ltd, and had been producing soft toys, teddy bears and dolls since their Chiltern Toy Works at Chesham was established in 1908. Their own range of Chiltern vinyl dolls was produced from 1958 to 1967.

The company did not make composition dolls or hard plastic dolls, but in the mid-Forties Chiltern Toys held a contract as sole selling agents of a range of hard plastic dolls made by Nene Plastics. They introduced several of these Rosebud-type dolls into their own toy range in the early Fifties, presumably to coincide with the coronation.

Maker: Chiltern
Doll name: none
Size: 7"/18cm
Marks: 'England' across the small of the back
Date: early 1950s

Three fully-jointed Chiltern costume-type dolls showing the three hair colours of blonde, brunette and auburn glued-on, curled wigs. They had sleeping eyes and these three were purchased naked for dressing at home.

Many companies produced a few dolls in that year dressed in coronation robes, or just as British costume dolls. The Chiltern hard plastic dolls were 7" tall, had blue sleeping eyes and elastic-strung jointed limbs. They were supplied with glued-on rayon wigs in several colours – pale blonde, fair, auburn, brunette and black – and were sold naked as well as dressed as costume dolls. The dolls were marked 'ENGLAND' across the small of the back, and the costumes included Welsh, Scottish and national costumes from around the world. Particularly attractive were the black versions dressed in African and Indian costumes.

By 1958 Chiltern was producing PVC (poly-vinyl-chloride) dolls. In less than ten years they made a range of small quality dolls which included little girl types with unusual character faces, babies and teenage girls, all with saran nylon rooted hair and quality heavy-weight bodies. It is often said that you can tell a Chiltern doll by the weight of its body.

In 1967, on the retirement of their managing director, the Chiltern Company was sold to Chad Valley and soon after being acquired, doll production ceased.

◄ PAGE 28
Maker: Chiltern (H. G. Stone & Co Ltd)
Doll name: **Miniature & Costume Dolls**
Size: 7"/18cm
Marks: 'England'
Date: early 1950s

These miniatures were unusual in that they were fully jointed and could be purchased either for dressing at home or in a wide variety of national costumes.

This illustration on the left shows the naked five-jointed body of the Chiltern 7" costume type dolls. Notice also the painted shoes.

Maker: Chiltern
Doll name: **Costume Doll**
Size: 7"/18cm
Marks: 'England' across the small of the back
Date: early 1950s

This blonde girl is dressed in Austrian national costume.

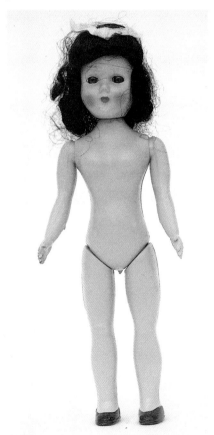

Makers: House of Nisbet Ltd and Almar
Dolls Ltd
Doll name: **Welsh/Irish/Scottish
Costume Dolls**
Size: 7"/18cm
Marks: None on Nisbet, just a wrist tag;
'Almar Dolls Made in Eng'
Date: 1960s

Many National Costume dolls were made
throughout the 1950s and 1960s in hard
plastic. Many were unmarked and are now
untraceable.

Costume and miscellaneous dolls

Costume dolls were produced by many companies in England especially in the early Fifties at the time of the coronation of Queen Elizabeth II. Unfortunately, very many were unmarked and were only made for a few years, so are not now very easy to trace. One often sees large quantities of these dolls in boxes under stalls at collector fairs, swapmeets or on shelves in second hand shops that no one seems interested in. It is however worth a careful look as one might come across a marked one and be able to identify or attribute it to a particular company. A friend came across a lovely little composition Forties girl in this way, and on close inspection discovered that it was marked 'HS 220' on its back. This mark was used by H. Schelhorn & Co. Ltd who formed their company in the mid-Forties in Leicester. The firm made composition dolls through the late Forties, Fifties and Sixties, switching to vinyl in the Seventies and Eighties. Hard plastic dolls were never made by the company, today known as Telitoy and still a family-run business.

Maker: Tudor Rose
Doll names: unkown
Sizes: 5"/12.5cm, 8"/20cm
Marks: Three centre dolls: 'Tudor Rose Made in England'. Two larger dolls 'Made in England'
Date: 1950s and early 1960s

The centre doll is a crawling baby with painted features, that actually crawls along. The two little boys have sleeping eyes and jointed limbs. The two larger 8"/20cm dolls have sleeping eyes and jointed limbs and identical hands to the two marked 'Tudor Rose' boys. This company was famous for making dolls' houses and furniture through the 1950s but also made other small dolls and toys of hard plastic.

◀ **PAGE 32**
TOP LEFT
Maker: Marcol
Doll name: **Fairy**
Size: 7"/18cm
Marks: none
Date: 1950s

This company distributed dolls throughout the 1950s but they are difficult to attribute once the clothing and packaging has been lost.

◀ **BELOW**
This assorted group of costume dolls includes two 6"/15cm Bronwyn Welsh costume dolls, on the left; a Chiltern 7"/18cm Austrian girl in the centre; second from right an unmarked African lady with her little jointed piccaninny, and right an unmarked English-made bride. All the dolls, with the exception of the Chiltern, have one-piece bodies and moving arms.

◀ **PAGE 32**
TOP RIGHT
Maker: unknown, but probably made in the British Empire
Doll names: unknown
Sizes: 5"/12.5cm
Marks: 'Codeg dolls' on box
Date: 1950s

Cowan De Groot, London Importers, used the name Codeg when marketing dolls through the 1950s. These dolls have been included as it is very unusual to find a boxed set of seven dolls all still in their original clothes and shoes. The dolls are of hard plastic with sleeping eyes and jointed limbs. (Collection Christine Wimsey)

BELOW LEFT
Maker: Kleeware
Doll name: **Thumbsuck Baby**
Size: 2¹/₂"/6.5cm
Marks: 'Kleeware England' on back
Date: 1950s

These one-piece thumbsuck babies were made in several sizes between 2¹/₂"/6.5cm and 5¹/₂"/13cm tall with moulded hair and painted features. Kleeware made miniature Kiddies Playset furniture in white plastic and tiny one-inch rubbery plastic babies in the 1950s and 1960s.

BELOW RIGHT
Maker: Schelhorn S
Doll name: none
Size: 5¹/₂"/13cm
Marks: 'HS 220' on back
Date: through the 1940s

A lovely little girl doll with moulded 1940s-style hair. Made of composition and fully jointed, with painted features and shoes. (Collection Christine Wimsey)

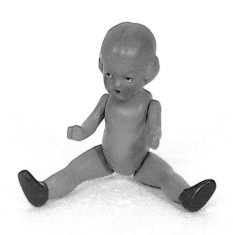

Many doll enthusiasts have collected costume dolls over the years as they are small enough to display in a cabinet or stand on a small window ledge. The latter practice is not really to be recommended as bright sunlight fades and disintegrates their costumes and eventually the plastic of the doll itself, although I know many who keep them in this way as they like to look at them.

In this section I have identified perhaps the most popular and more easily found specimens from this hard plastic costume era.

Maker: Almar Dolls Ltd
Doll name: **Scottish Costume Doll**
Size: 7"/18cm
Marks: 'Almar Dolls Made in England' across back
Date: 1960s

One of the attractive range of British costume dolls made from hard plastic with glued-on wigs, straight, non-bending legs and jointed, elastic-strung arms. The face slightly resembles the Chiltern costume dolls.

Almar Dolls Ltd

1964 THROUGH THE SEVENTIES

Founded in East London in the early Sixties, this company used a derivative of the directors' first names – Albert and Mary Dorsett – as its trademark.

They manufactured a large range of traditional costume dolls through the Sixties and Seventies which included brides, Scottish, Welsh and Irish costumes, London cockneys, Union Jack dolls, beefeaters, policemen, soldiers and kings and queens of England, as well as costumes from around the world. The dolls were 7" and 8" tall with a glued-on wig, sleeping eyes, jointed elastic strung arms and straight, non-bending legs. The faces slightly resembled the Chiltern costume dolls made by Nene Plastics. Almar Dolls were all marked on their backs 'Almar Dolls. Made in England'.

Peggy Nisbet Ltd/ House of Nisbet Ltd

1953 TO 1990

Peggy Nisbet started making dolls at home in Weston-Super-Mare in 1953. To commemorate the coronation she made a limited edition 7" model of HM Queen Elizabeth II. Soon other miniature dolls followed, and a company and workshop were set up in 1956, the latter being destroyed by fire in 1970.

After a new factory was built, her range increased to include 7" figures of historical characters, Hollywood film stars and many, many more collectors' dolls. Various media were used, including bisque, styrene composition, plastic, porcelain, vinyl, wax and wood. The dolls illustrated here are costume dolls and ballerinas of hard plastic composition and each has a glued-on mohair wig of various colours, blue or brown painted eyes, arms that move and legs in a fixed position. This range made in the late Sixties and early Seventies portrays English, Welsh, Irish and Scottish girls, schoolgirls with plaits, dancers and ballerinas. Each one has the socks/stockings and shoes painted on. The dolls are unmarked but the wrist tag on the Welsh girl illustrated states 'Happy Dolls Made in England'.

In the Seventies, soft toys for children were made by this company, including a 'golly', Beatrix Potter toys and teddy bears. The Eighties saw a range of vinyl 'My Little Girl' fashion dolls.

Maker: House of Nisbet
Doll name: **Ballerina**
Size: 7"/18cm
Marks: none
Date: 1960s

These lovely ballerinas of hard plastic composition have glued-on wigs in various colours, and legs in a fixed position with arms that move. Their features, shoes and socks are painted on. They came dressed in a variety of pretty pink or white ballet dresses.

Maker: House of Nisbet
Doll name: **Irish Dancer**
Size: 7"/18cm
Marks: none
Date: 1960s

Very similar to the ballerinas above, these dancers are dressed in traditional costumes.

Maker: House of Nisbet
Doll name: **English Flower Girl**
Size: 8"/20cm
Marks: none. Wrist tag 'Costume Dolls by Peggy Nisbet'
Date: 1960s and 1970s

This **English Flower Girl** represents an English national costume. The doll has a fixed body with jointed arms, glued-on wig and painted features. She carries a basket of 'English flowers'.

Maker: House of Nisbet
Doll name: **Welsh National Costume**
Size: 7"/18cm
Marks: none. Wrist tag 'Happy Dolls England'
Date: 1960s

Hard plastic composition with one-piece body and legs, jointed arms and painted features. The doll has a black mohair wig and wears a Welsh national costume.

Rexard (Exports) Ltd

1960s TO THE PRESENT DAY

This export company distributes small costume dolls from their Brighton works. Mostly national and historical costume dolls in 7" and 8" sizes were imported by them and are marked 'Empire Made'. All the dolls have the same basic face but the costumes are varied and offer many different characters. Each one has a swing ticket which describes the figure being portrayed, gives the name of the designer Odette Arden and a list of the other designs available – some 40 national costumes and 20 historical costumes. The dolls themselves were of hard plastic and fixed to their stand as they were not for undressing, the clothes being attached to the doll and trimmed with beads and jewels to portray the beautiful historical costumes. They were sold in thousands of outlets throughout Britain and were fairly inexpensive so that one could form a large collection without too much outlay. Later dolls were made from vinyl and were more suitable as play dolls, having painted features, rooted hair and movable limbs. They still carried a swing ticket, the dolls themselves being unmarked.

QUEEN OF SCOTLAND AND DISPUTED
SUCCESSOR TO THE ENGLISH THRONE

Maker: Rexard
Doll names: **Mary Queen of Scots, Scottish Girl**
Sizes: 7"/18cm and 8"/20cm
Marks: 'Mary Queen of Scotts' and historical note on base of stand. Swing ticket: 'Costume Dolls by Rexard'
Date: 1960s and 1970s

On the left a hard plastic Empire Made fixed-position doll. Her clothes are jewelled and fixed in place. On the right a vinyl costume doll with removable clothes from the same company, a decade apart.

Rogark Manufacturing Co.

1950s AND 1960s

Maker: Rogark
Doll name: **Costume Dolls**
Size: 7"/18cm tall
Marks: 'Rogark Made in Wales UK' across the backs
Date: 1950s and 1960s

The two dolls on the left are a Scottish boy and girl, on the right an Irish girl and a Scottish piper. The dolls have a one-piece body with jointed arms, glued-on wigs for girls and moulded hair for boys. All have sleeping eyes and painted shoes.

Mr G. Rogers started his small company in 1950 making Welsh, Scottish, Irish and many other national costume dolls from his base at Penmaenmawr in North Wales.

These attractive little 7" hard plastic dolls had distinctive hands and faces with moulded hair for boys and mohair wigs for the girls. They had sleeping eyes and movable arms and were marked 'Rogark Made in Wales UK' on their backs. In 1953 Rogark introduced 3" tall 'Television Topper Dolls' modelled on the popular TV dancers. Available separately or in boxed sets of 12, they wore the famous uniforms with top hat and cane. Different hair colours were available.

After Mr Roger's death, his wife took over the running of the company which has since closed.

Doll Industries Ltd

This little-known North London-based doll manufacturer registered the name 'Doll-in-Doll' for their hard plastic dolls in 1948. However, many of their dolls were unmarked and therefore are difficult to find and attribute, as once the box has been destroyed the doll becomes unidentifiable. Some of their hard plastic dolls were marked 'D.I.L. Made in England' across the back of the doll and 'Doll-in-Doll Made in England' on the box.

The company used the same London distributor for their dolls as D.G. Todd's 'Roddy' doll company during the late Forties and, whether by coincidence or not, many of the Doll-in-Dolls resembled the 'Roddy' doll. Making a lovely range of composition and hard plastic girl dolls, the company used traditional methods in their doll-making. They had sleeping eyes and glued-on wigs in various styles and colours. A range of hand-assisted walkie-talkie dolls was also made with ma-ma voice box and grille in the back. All were dressed in attractive ribbon- and lace-trimmed dresses and bonnets. Presumably naked dolls for dressing at home were also made, but as no actual samples have come to hand I cannot verify this.

By the late Fifties the company was producing vinyl dolls, introducing a range of dressed teenage dolls which included a fairy with wand, a bride and various attractive gala evening dresses, all beautifully trimmed with lace and ribbons. Their later boxes were also particularly appealing, being decorated with a ribbon design, a teddy bear and a doll intertwined with 'Made in England Doll-in-Doll'. Early composition dolls were in plain brown boxes with only a Doll-in-Doll label on one end of the box.

Maker: Doll Industries Ltd
Doll name: unknown
Size: 24"/61cm
Marks: 'DIL Made in England' across back
Date: 1950

An attractive hand-assisted walking-talking doll with ma-ma voice box and grille in her back. She has a golden brown nylon wig, sleeping blue eyes with painted blue-grey eyeshadow and lovely rosy cheeks. Her body and legs are slim and she wears her original clothes and shoes.
(Collection Christine Wimsey)

Maker: Doll Industries Ltd
Doll name: **Madame Pompadour**
Size: 20"/51cm
Marks: None on composition dolls. The plain brown carton is labelled 'Doll In Doll Made in England'
Date: 1948

This company made many attractive, elaborately dressed composition dolls in the late 1940s with waisted bodies and a similar face and mohair wig, sleeping eyes, open-closed mouth and teeth. The composition dolls were unmarked and have become extremely hard to find and attribute. The one illustrated here still has her original clothes, shoes and box and is dressed in three layers of calico undies and a satin two-tone dress with leatherette shoes.

Maker: Doll Industries Ltd
Doll name: **Fairy**
Size: 20"/51cm
Marks: none on doll. 'Made in England Doll-in-Doll' on box
Date: late 1950s

This lovely teenage 'vinyl' doll has rooted fair hair, sleeping eyes and wears her original clothes of a 'fairy'. She stands in front of her original box and she came with a 'wand'. Although not hard plastic she has been included to show the box. Without the box these Doll Industries Ltd dolls are very difficult to find and identify. (Collection Christine Wimsey)

This diagram shows the inside workings of the Doll Industries walking-talking doll with no visible mechanism. They were constructed in a similar way to the Roddy slimmer walkie dolls, the arms being strung independently from the legs.

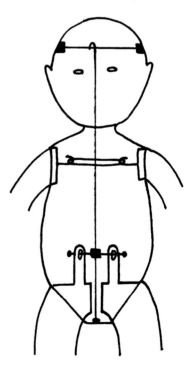

Faerie Glen/
Hook & Franks

1964 TO THE PRESENT DAY

Peggy Franks (now Mrs Hook) and her mother founded this company in Walthamstow, north London in 1964, using a team of outworkers to make a range of dolls' clothes to fit every conceivable size of doll in a varied assortment of ensembles from bedtime, daytime, beach, sports and uniforms to cocktail and evening wear. Many had added accessories and were individually packed with their distinctive 'Faerie Glen' header card.

The company did not make its own dolls, but its first introductions were the English-made hard plastic **Tonie** and **Sally** twins, using the similar Miss Rosebud-type mould in the early Sixties. Unlike **Miss Rosebud**, **Roddy** and Amanda Jane's **Jinx**, these twins were completely unmarked and are quite difficult to find today. (It is thought by many collectors that the dolls were made in either the Rosebud or Roddy factories, but I have been unable to find proof of this. **Tonie**, with a long-haired wig in three colourways of brunette, auburn or blonde, was priced at four shillings and elevenpence undressed in the mid-Sixties, and **Sally** with short hair wig in the same three colours, was four shillings and sixpence. Their little booklet, *Faerie Glen Wear presents Tonie and Sally*, depicted 40 different outfits that could be purchased separately for these hard plastic twins. Also shown were a pink painted wooden 'wardrobe with six hangers' and a washable plastic-coated 'doll's trousseau case' containing a selection of clothes to cover 24 hours in a twin doll's busy day!

The dolls themselves were 8" tall, with a cute face, painted lips and sleeping blue eyes without lashes, and five posable joints. Faerie Glen continued to produce clothes for a number of vinyl dolls, including their Sindy-lookalike teenage **Tina** in the late Sixties, their larger teens **Gigi**, **Jackie** and **Mimi** also in the Sixties, and many baby and toddler dolls made for them in countries around the world. Only the clothes were actually made in Britain.

◀ PAGE 42
Maker: Faerie Glen/Hook & Franks
Doll names: **Tonie and Sally**
Size: 8"/20 cm
Marks: none
Date: mid-1960s

Many collectors believe that the companies of Rosebud or Roddy made dolls for Hook & Franks, as the company did not make their own dolls – only the outfits. However, I have never been able to verify this and it is reasonable to assume that they bought dolls from both. Their huge range of outfits in many sizes is world famous.

Maker: Faerie Glen
Doll name: **Tonie and Sally Twins**
Size: 8"
Marks: none
Date: mid-1960s

Tonie with long brunette hair wig on the left and Sally with short auburn hair wig on the right.

Original booklet 'Faerie Glen Wear presents Tonie and Sally' which accompanied the dolls and depicted 40 different outfits available for these twins.

Morris Mitchell & Co Ltd/ Mitchell Plastics Ltd/ Mitchell & Hardy Ltd

1945 TO 1967

This small plastics company, based in Dalston (East London), started out in 1940 making acetate doll masks, cycle mudguards, eye shields, lampshades, dart flights, novelties, etc, followed by anti-gas goggles, gas mask cases and identity card cases for the war. Their trademark 'Mormit', was derived from the directors' surnames.

While experimenting with PVC for a doll face mask, managing director Mr F.G. Mitchell discovered that he could make a complete doll from this substance, and produced his first doll in 1945 using a domestic oven. He obtained patents in the same year for this construction method and two more for an eye socket and a moving eye. Similar patents were applied for by Cascelloid at the same time and by tacit consent both companies took no action against the other. Objections were raised, however, by German and Swiss firms who had been making similar dolls since 1936, but the Mitchell doll was in fact of a different construction. Thus it was that Mr F.G. Mitchell's doll totally changed the doll industry, as most other dolls made in the post-war years had elastic-strung limbs. The Mitchell 'Mormit' doll was a drink-and-wet doll and could be bathed in water, fed by bottle and have its nappy changed. No elastic bands, discs or hooks were used. Judging from the large quantity of dolls which have survived the last 45 years, the company's claims for their dolls' indestructibility seem true.

The first series of dolls produced by the firm were the 'Marie' series described as 'Dolls of the Future' and were made of soft skin-like plastic with jointed socket limbs that could be taken apart and popped back together or replaced easily. The first two dolls to be produced in 1945 were **Marie José**, 9" tall, and **Marie Valerie**, 13" tall, named after Mr F.G. Mitchell's daughters who were then both little girls. Soon to follow, in 1946, were **Marie Mia**, 11" tall, and **Marie Lou**, 15" tall. **Marie Ann** in 1947 at 24" tall was the largest of the Marie series of five dolls and was sold specifically as a maternity baby care training doll to the then London County Council. She had the weight of a real baby and could be bathed in water just like the other four in the series. All five dolls in the 'Marie' series had fixed glassene-type eyes, and were marked across their shoulders 'Marie

Maker: Morris Mitchell/Mitchell Plastics/ Mitchell & Hardy Ltd
Doll name: **Marie José**
Size: 9"/23cm
Marks: 'Marie José Pro Pat 30189/45' Pro Pat 31718/47 across shoulders. 'Mormit Product Made in England' across small of back
Date: late 1940s

The smallest doll in the Marie series was named after one of Mr F.G. Mitchell's daughters and first made in 1945. She is a soft plastic (PVC) drink-and-wet doll with moulded head and glassene-type eyes. She can be bathed in water, taken apart and put together again easily. This doll revolutionised the doll industry and was pioneered by Mr F.G. Mitchell when other dolls of this period were hook and elastic strung.

Maker: Morris Mitchell/Mitchell Plastics/
Mitchell & Hardy Ltd
Doll names: **Marie Ann/Marie Valerie**
Sizes: 24"/61cm, 13"/33cm
Marks: 'Marie Ann Pro Pat 30199/46, Pro
Pat 31718/47', 'Marie/Valerie, Pro Pat
30189/45, Mormit Product, Made in
England'
Dates: 1948, 1946

Marie Ann was also made in black and a
large number of these bigger dolls were
sold to the London County Council as a
maternity baby care training doll. Made of
soft plastic PVC she could be bathed in
water and taken apart and reassembled.
She had pale blue glassene-type fixed eyes
and an open-closed mouth with two
painted teeth. Marie Valerie was named
after one of Mr F. G. Mitchell's daughters.
Both models are quite hard to find today.

name pro pat 30189/45' (which denoted the year the original patent was applied for) 'pro pat 31718/47' (which denoted the year the model was made) and across the small of the back 'Mormit Product Made in England' (which denoted the company's trademark).

The company opened a new factory in 1947 under the name of Mitchell Plastics Ltd and acquired premises in Wood Green, London N22. After the announcement at Buckingham Palace of the birth of the heir to the throne, HRH Prince Charles, a new series of dolls was introduced in 1949 in commemoration of that event, and called **Prince Charming** (15" tall), **Baby Prince Charming** (11" tall) and **Princess Linda** (16" tall). These dolls were made and marked in the same way as the Marie series, except **Princess Linda** who had the same PVC head but a latex skin type body filled with foam rubber. Each doll had a different face and size. If you wish to date your dolls more accurately, Mr R.G. Mitchell has pointed out that early dolls pre-1948 were fitted with glass eyes and later dolls with a composite eye, with a printed iris and a transparent cover, set in a metal cleated cup. Their factory of origin can be ascertained from initials moulded onto the outside neck flange concealed by the head when fitted in place. All marks commenced after October 1948 and were WG for Wood Green, D for Dalston or BS for Bishops Stortford, where the company opened another factory under the name of Mitchell & Hardy Plastics in 1949.

However, after the factories were closed down during the early Sixties, only the moulds from Wood Green were used and the marks were ground off the other moulds. They continued to make the dolls plus small Mormit unnamed dolls, novelties, small plastic Wendy dolls, pixie dolls, floating ducks and fishes and plastic balls in several sizes. No more than 100 people worked for the company at any one time. They also researched and made many household items, such as plastic plumbing, sink traps, pipes, guttering, as well as PVC gloves and other PVC fabric coverings.

Mr F.G. Mitchell made no attempt to install rotary casting methods to mechanise their doll production, preferring to concentrate on the household items at that time. The dolls were still made by hand through the Fifties, but, sadly, all doll production was closed down by the mid-Sixties leaving the company to continue making household and commercial products which were more viable and profitable for the company.

Maker: Morris Mitchell/Mitchell Plastics/Mitchell & Hardy Ltd
Doll name: **Marie Lou**
Size: 15"/38cm
Marks: 'Marie Lou Pro Pat 30199/46' across shoulders. 'Mormit Product Made in England' across small of back
Date: late 1940s

First made in 1946, she also had moulded hair, glassene-type eyes and a soft PVC body with head and limbs that could be taken apart and put back together like the others in the Marie series.

Maker: Morris Mitchell/Mitchell Plastics/Mitchell & Hardy Ltd
Doll name: **Marie Mia**
Size: 11"/28cm
Marks: 'Marie Mia Pro Pat 30189/45 Pro Pat 31718/47' across back.
'Mormit Product Made in England' across small of back
Date: late 1940s

This drink-and-wet doll followed the others in 1946 and was made in the same way with moulded hair and glassene-type eyes.

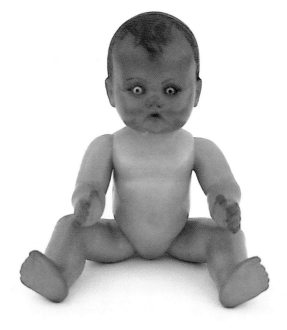

Maker: Morris Mitchell/Mitchell Plastics/Mitchell & Hardy Ltd
Doll name: **Prince Charming**
Size: 13"/33cm
Marks: 'Prince Charming MP'
Date: 1948

Prince Charming was made in exactly the same way as the Marie series but with sleeping eyes. A smaller 11" version was also made.

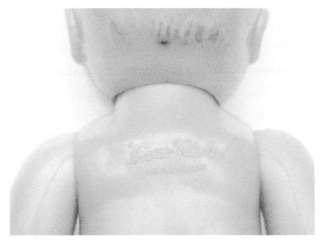

'Marie Valerie, Pro Pat 30189/45' denoted the year the patent was taken out: 1945. 'Mormit Product Made in England' denoted the company's trademark.

The limbs and head could easily be taken apart and then push-fitted together again. This revolutionary method of construction for a doll was pioneered by Mr F.G. Mitchell in 1945.

Palitoy Ltd (Cascelloid)

1919 TO THE MID 1980s

As a young man in 1919, Mr Alfred Edward Pallett started the company called Cascelloid Ltd in Leicester, making celluloid toys and novelties. Their first one-piece-bodied doll with movable arms was made in 1925. She was called **Diddums** and made from moulded celluloid in three sizes. Many more small novelty celluloid dolls followed including girls, boys, babies, sailors, **Rags** and **Bubbles**. During the late Twenties Kewpie Dolls were added to their range, and during the late Thirties the company became a subsidiary of British Xylonite Ltd and two new materials for dolls were used. 'Bexoid' was introduced in 1937, which was light like celluloid but non-flammable and used for toys, heads on dolls with soft bodies, novelties, Bexoid cherubs and Walt Disney characters. 'Plastex' in 1938 was heavy like composition, but unbreakable, as a kind of glue was used to give the material elasticity. By the late Thirties larger dolls were being moulded in two halves by injection-moulded Plastex, then joined together leaving a seam lengthwise down the sides of the body. One named doll in 1938, was **Priscilla**, an 18" girl toddler with moulded hair, painted features

ABOVE AND LEFT
Maker: Cascelloid Ltd/Palitoy
Doll name: **Priscilla**
Size: 18"/46cm
Marks: 'Plastex' on back of head, 'Made in England' across shoulders
Date: 1938

A type of composition doll made with a glue that retained its elasticity, creating an unbreakable material for doll-making. She is a striking doll with moulded hair, painted eyes and elastic strung limbs. The hands are unusual in as much as all the fingers are moulded together, leaving the thumb separate. The plain carton with Plastex Doll label is the box in which she was purchased.
(Collection Christine Wimsey)

Maker: Cascelloid Ltd/Palitoy Ltd
Doll names: **Fairytale Doll, Walking Doll, Patsy Drink and Wet Doll**
Sizes: 15"/38cm, 15"/38cm, 20"/51cm
Marks: 'Palitoy, Made in England'; 'Palitoy Made in England'; 'Patsy' on back of head, 'Brit Pat 600270 Made in England'
Dates: 1955, 1952, 1952

Palitoy made fewer hard plastic models than Pedigree as they were also pioneering the use of rubbery vinyl for dolls. Several versions of Patsy were issued as early as 1948 and were updated almost annually with collectors finding specimens with various different patent numbers. Here, Patsy has her original bottle and knitted outfit from contemporary patterns produced and printed by women's magazines of the day.

and jointed, bent limbs. Her hands were unusual with all the fingers moulded together and a separate thumb. She came wearing a floral cotton dress and pants trimmed in white with white socks. This doll was also available in black plastic. Other Plastex dolls at this time had a moulded head only with cloth bodies.

The name Palitoy was first used at this time and registered as the company's trademark in 1940. During the war years the factory at Coalville, as with most other companies, was requisitioned for the war effort to make munitions. As war ended, Mr Pallett, managing direc-tor, founder and company namesake, retired, although he always kept a close interest in the company. After the war the first-injection moulded cellulose acetate (hard plastic) toys and dolls were made and the company's Coalville factory was officially opened. It was during these years that the company was also pioneering and experimenting with rubbery plastic dolls, an early form of vinyl. Several named dolls were made in this softer medium, including **Rock-a-bye-baby** in the early Forties. A 22" baby doll with moulded hair and sleeping eyes, which came dressed in a satin gown. **Patsy**, a rubbery plastic doll in a dull flesh colour (in the late Forties), was a baby doll 15" tall with moulded hair, fixed glassene-type eyes with lashes, fingers moulded

LEFT
Maker: Cascelloid Ltd/Palitoy
Doll name: **Patsy**
Size: 15"/38cm
Marks: 'Patsy Palitoy' on back of head. 'Brit Pat 600270 Made in England' across back
Date: 1952

This Patsy is made of hard imitation rubber. Note that she has a hole through the lips to take a dummy, as she is a drink-and-wet doll.

RIGHT
Maker: Cascelloid Ltd/Palitoy
Doll name: **Drink and Wet Baby 'Patsy'**
Size: 15"/38cm
Marks: 'Made in England Pat No 535811' on back of neck. 'Brit Pat 600270 Made in England' across back
Date: 1958

This doll has the same body as the earlier rubbery Patsy but is made of a soft PVC plastic with push-fit limbs. The head is of hard plastic, with moulded hair, sleeping eyes and a hole through the lips.

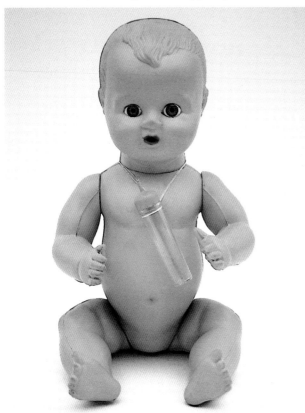

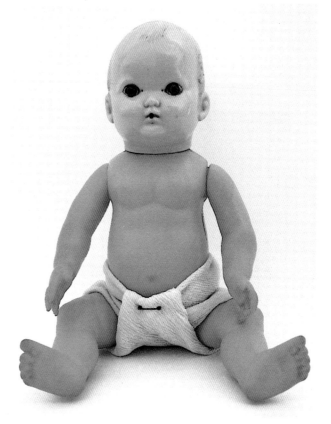

Maker: Cascelloid Ltd/Palitoy
Doll name: **Drink and Wet Baby 'Treasure Babe'**
Size: 18"/46cm
Marks: 'Palitoy Made in England' on back of neck
Date: 1958

Another soft PVC plastic baby with push-fit limbs inside his original box. The head is also soft with moulded hair, sleeping eyes and a hole through the lips to take a dummy. He wears his original nappy.

Maker: Cascelloid Ltd/Palitoy
Doll name: unknown but she is a **Pin-Up** type Cat No. 5547
Size: 14"/35.5cm
Marks: none on doll
Date: 1950

These hard plastic dolls were available in several sizes and had glued-on mohair wigs which could be curled, brushed and combed as these items were provided in her box. This one is a walking doll with sleeping eyes and an unusual mechanism which is hidden in the body. On the front of the box it states 'Palitoy Perfection'!
(Collection Christine Wimsey)

together with a separate thumb and a drink-and-wet feature. She was also available in a dull black version and marked 'Patsy' Palitoy on the back of her neck 'Pat 600270 Made in England' on her back, which referred to her body mould which was used later on other dolls as well.

Other soft plastic babies in the early Fifties were of a pinker colour and came dressed in a nappy as they were drink-and-wet dolls too, with jointed socket limbs that needed no discs, hooks or elastic bands. Made from the same body mould and also called **Patsy**, these babies had hard plastic heads in the early Fifties and softer vinyl heads by 1956 and were also made in black when **Patsy Anne** in smaller sizes of 9", 11" and 13" with a bath set were also introduced. During the early Fifties, Palitoy was experimenting with many different plastic/vinyl materials calling them 'petal skin' and also many types of doll. Perhaps this is the reason why there are not quite so many hard plastic dolls in their range as some of their competitors.

A lovely variety of hard plastic dolls were on display however in the late Forties and early Fifties, including babies, toddlers, girls with open and closed mouths and walking talking girl dolls in various sizes and styles with mohair glued-on wigs as well as moulded hair babies. Their dolls had pretty facial expressions and many had teeth. Those worth a mention were **Pin-Up** type girls in 14" to 25" sizes with a brush and comb for their brushable hair supplied in their box. This model was also available as the **Girl Walking Doll** and advertised in the *Girl* comic during the mid-Fifties, with twelve 'Style' dressmaking patterns available separately for her which included a party dress, day dress, blouse and skirt among others.

20", hand-assisted walking-talking dolls were unusual with head,

Maker: Cascelloid Ltd/Palitoy
Doll name: **Pin-Up Doll**
Size: 15"/38cm
Marks: Palitoy Made in England
Date: 1955

This Pin-Up series was introduced with storybook and fairytale themes etc. The dress she is wearing is marked 'Palitoy Playthings Made in England'.

Maker: Palitoy
Doll name: **Pin-Up Girl**
Size: 25"/64cm
Marks: 'Palitoy Made in England'
Date: 1950

A lovely large walking doll similar to that at far left. Originally purchased in a floral cotton dress, she now wears a pale blue cotton cord pinafore and toning check blouse. A brush and comb for her hair came in her box.

This advertisement appeared in *Girl* magazine for children in 1955 advertising the lovely clothes that could be made up at home from the 'Style' paper patterns available through the magazine. The *Girl* doll was made by Palitoy in 1953 and was a **Pin-Up** type.

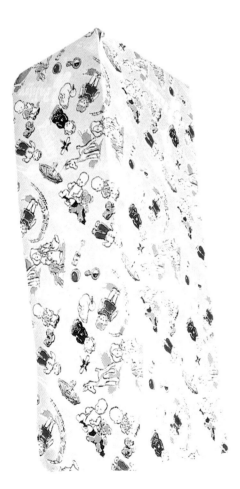

Lovely clothes for your GIRL doll

*I*F you are lucky enough to own a GIRL Walking Doll, you can have hours of fun making a whole wardrobe of smart clothes for her to wear. All our specially designed patterns are very quick and easy to sew and you will find an outfit for every occasion in our range of twelve lovely styles. Choose from these styles:—

- *Style No. 1 – a party dress*
- *Style No. 2 – a blouse and skirt*
- *Style No. 3 – sun dress and stole*
- *Style No. 4 – a cape and hat*
- *Style No. 5 – slacks, shorts and blouse*
- *Style No. 6 – a day dress*
- *Style No. 7 – slip and knicker set*
- *Style No. 8 – a bloomer suit*
- *Style No. 9 – bridesmaid's dress and petticoat*
- *Style No. 10 – a square dancing outfit*
- *Style No. 11 – a nightdress*
- *Style No. 12 – Hawaiian fancy dress*

This is style No. 3, a sun dress with a matching stole.

How to send for the patterns

Write to : – GIRL Doll Patterns, Long Lane, Aintree, Liverpool 9, enclosing your postal order value 10d (made payable to Hulton Press Ltd., and crossed '& Co') stating clearly which style you want. If you would like more than one, don't forget to increase the value of your postal order by 10d for every extra GIRL doll pattern that you require.

Each pattern costs 10d, including postage. Remember, though, that they will fit only the GIRL walking doll made by Palitoy.

Lovely clothes for your GIRL doll

*I*F you are lucky enough to own a GIRL Walking Doll, you can have hours of fun making a whole wardrobe of smart clothes for her to wear. All our specially designed patterns are very quick and easy to sew and you will find an outfit for every occasion in our range of twelve lovely styles. Choose from these styles: –

- *Style No. 1 – a party dress*
- *Style No. 2 – a blouse and skirt*
- *Style No. 3 – sun dress and stole*
- *Style No. 4 – a cape and hat*
- *Style No. 5 – slacks, shorts and blouse*
- *Style No. 6 – a day dress*
- *Style No. 7 – slip and knicker set*
- *Style No. 8 – a bloomer suit*
- *Style No. 9 – bridesmaid's dress and petticoat*
- *Style No. 10 – a square dancing outfit*
- *Style No. 11 – a nightdress*
- *Style No. 12 – Hawaiian fancy dress*

This is style No. 7 in our pattern range, a slip and knicker set – and there are eleven more styles to choose from!

How to send for the patterns

Write to : – GIRL Doll Patterns, Long Lane, Aintree, Liverpool 9, enclosing your postal order value 10d (made payable to Hulton Press Ltd. and crossed '&/Co') stating clearly which style you want. If you would like more than one, don't forget to increase the value of your postal order by 10d for every extra GIRL doll pattern that you require.

Each pattern costs 10d, including postage. Remember, though, that they will fit only the GIRL walking doll made by Palitoy.

A typical 1950s style box from Palitoy decorated with dollies, teddies and toys. This box was introduced around 1950 and was used for a few years.

arms and legs that moved in unison as they were walked along – almost in a marching action. These dolls had flirting, sleeping eyes, a short mohair wig, which resembled a Thirties' style, and rather short legs. They were sometimes referred to as 'Belinda' dolls.

Fashion dolls, 7", 14" and 16" tall, in a very shiny plastic with mohair wigs, had lovely mauve eyes and slimmer, straight-legged, jointed bodies with fingers moulded together. Many of the smaller sizes came dressed in British or Scottish costumes, or as brides, ballerinas, etc. Character dolls were also produced, Peter Brough's **Archie Andrews** ventriloquist doll being a popular one due to the radio programme 'Educating Archie', throughout the Fifties. The doll had a hard plastic head, hands and feet, painted features and was advertised as suitable for boys or girls – easy to work!

The signature on the back of the Palitoy dolls does not have the same flourish as those of some of their competitors'. It is merely 'Palitoy Made in England' in capitals marked on the back of the neck or sometimes across the shoulders too.

By 1956, Palitoy had introduced a 'petal skin' range of dolls which had hard plastic heads and a new vinyl soft skin body which in some models was stuffed with hygienic filling. **Pretty baby** in 1957 came

ABOVE LEFT
Maker: Cascelloid Ltd/Palitoy
Doll name: **Girl Dress Me Walking Doll**
Size: 15"/38cm
Date: 1953

This **Pin-Up** style doll is shown with her original box which states that she walks, sleeps, stands, and sits. Her magic hair can be washed, combed, curled. Notice the *Girl* head logo printed on her dress, pants and hair ribbon, also the buckle. The *Girl* comic was introduced in 1951 and ran throughout the 1950s and early 1960s.

ABOVE RIGHT
Maker: Cascelloid Ltd/Palitoy
Doll name: **Girl Dress Me Walking Doll**
Size: 15"/38cm
Date: 1953

These two show different wig colours. On the left is a blonde and on the right, auburn. The dolls were available in five hair colours: pale blonde, blonde, fair, auburn and brunette.

TOP LEFT
Maker: Cascelloid Ltd/Palitoy
Doll name: **Belinda**
Size: 20"/51cm
Marks: 'Palitoy Made in England'
Date: 1952

A walking-talking doll with the mechanism inside her body. She swings her arms, head and legs when walking in a marching action, has a ma-ma voice box with tiny grille in the stomach. The glued-on mohair wig on this doll is very reminiscent of the 1940s. Slightly out of proportion, her legs appear rather short.

TOP RIGHT
This diagram shows the hidden mechanism of Palitoy Walking Dolls, leaving the limbs smooth and free from screws and discs.

BELOW LEFT
Maker: Cascelloid Ltd/Palitoy
Doll name: **Paliglide Walking Dolls Penny**
Size: 21"/53cm
Marks: 'Palitoy Made in England'
Date: 1957

A hard plastic walking body with a vinyl rooted-hair head.

BELOW RIGHT
Maker: Cascelloid Ltd/Palitoy
Doll name: **Paliglide Walking Dolls Topsy**
Size: 21"/53cm
Marks: 'Palitoy Made in England'
Date: 1957

A hard plastic walker with amber sleeping eyes, hoop earrings and the unusual Palitoy marching action when walked along.

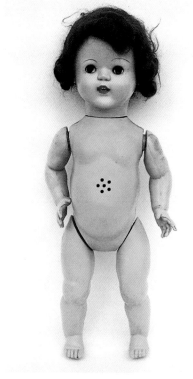

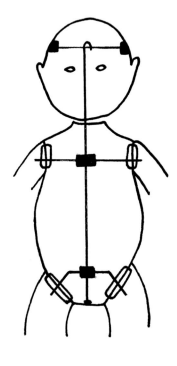

Maker: Cascelloid Ltd/Palitoy
Doll name: **Fashion Doll**
Size: 16"/40.5cm
Marks: 'Palitoy Made in England'
Date: early 1950s

These slimmer **Fashion Dolls** in a very shiny plastic with mohair wigs, lovely mauve eyes and slim straight legs were made in several sizes, 7", 14" and 16" tall. Many could be purchased dressed in British costumes.
(Collection Christine Wimsey)

The lower photograph shows the rather plain doll mark that appeared on all Palitoy hard plastic dolls.

Maker: Cascelloid Ltd/Palitoy
Doll name: **Archie Andrews**
Size: 12"/30.5cm
Marks: Palitoy
Date: early 1950s

More of a puppet than a doll, this is a good replica of Peter Brough's ventriloquist doll. He had a hard plastic head, hands and feet, painted features and was advertised as suitable for boys or girls – easy to work!
(Collection Christine Wimsey)

Maker: Cascelloid Ltd/Palitoy
Doll name: **Pretty Baby**
Size: 18"/46cm
Marks: 'Made in England' on back of neck
Date: 1957

Two of the lovely 'petal skin' dolls which had hard plastic heads and a new vinyl soft skin body which was stuffed with hygienic filling. This one has a blonde mohair ringlet curl wig, sleeping flirting eyes, and open closed mouth with teeth. She wears her original clothes and stands in the box in which she was sold.

with a blonde or brunette mohair ringlet curl wig, sleeping blue eyes and a red plastic dress, pants and bonnet. Her limbs were jointed and she stood 18" tall. **Belinda**, **Carol**, **Wendy**, **Miranda** and **Jennifer** were 17" girls with rooted hair in a ponytail style, while **Lindy** was the same size with a moulded ponytail. Another petal skin was a 12" boy dressed in a blue striped sunsuit, with glassene eyes and an attractive moulded hairstyle. Little girl versions were made too, as well as babies in four sizes. **Polly Pigtails**, the 10" hand puppet was also a petal skin doll and came dressed as a girl in a pink floral play-suit or a boy in a blue striped playsuit. The head, hands and feet were of vinyl soft skin and the playsuit was unstuffed so that the child's hand could work the puppet in a realistic way. Other such hand puppets were **Polly Hush-a-Bye**, a baby with soother, and a **Flower Pot Man**, a character taken from the Children's Hour television show of the time.

Also in 1957, Palitoy introduced **Paliglide Walking Dolls**: 21", 20" and 14" tall with a hard plastic body and the new rooted hair vinyl head. The range included named dolls **Sweet Sue** and **Penny**, both

ABOVE LEFT
Maker: Cascelloid Ltd/Palitoy
Doll name: **Pretty Baby**
Size: 18"/46cm
Marks: 'Made in England' on back of neck
Date: 1957

The same doll as illustrated left but with a brunette mohair curl wig. This photograph shows the end of her box, marked 'Soft Doll'.
(Collection Christine Wimsey)

LEFT
Maker: Cascelloid Ltd/Palitoy
Doll name: none
Size: 12"/30.5cm
Marks: 'Made in England'
Date: late 1950s

Another 'petal skin' series were the 12" little boys and girls. This one has moulded hair and glassene eyes. With jointed limbs, he stands next to his box which states 'It's a Palitoy Petal Skin Doll'.
(Collection Christine Wimsey)

ABOVE RIGHT
Maker: Cascelloid Ltd/Palitoy
Doll name: none
Size: 4"/10cm
Marks: 'Palitoy Made in England'
Date: early 1950s

Two tiny Palitoy dolls one with moulded hair and the other with a light brown mohair wig. Both fully jointed with painted sleeping eyes. Two of the many small novelty lines made by this company.

Maker: Cascelloid Ltd/Palitoy
Doll name: **Polly Pigtails**
Size: 10"/25.5cm
Marks: none
Date: 1952

Polly Pigtails was a hand puppet doll described on her box as 'Easy to work – Lifelike – Soft and cuddly – Behaves like a real baby'. She had petal skin head, hands and feet and the playsuit body was unstuffed so that the child's hand could work the puppet in a realistic way. (Collection Christine Wimsey)

RIGHT
Maker: Cascelloid Ltd/Palitoy
Doll name: **Polly Pigtails**
Size: 10"/25.5cm
Marks: none
Date: 1952

A blue Polly Pigtails showing blanket and original box.
(Collection Denise and Tony Slade)

21" tall, with open mouth and teeth. **Gillian**, **Sylvia** with sweet closed mouth expressions and black all plastic doll **Topsy**, all 20" tall, and **Tina**, 14" tall. All these Paliglide walking dolls were dressed in attractive removable dresses, panties, shoes and socks. These models spelt the end for hard plastic dolls, and the beginning of the vinyl era which saw many more innovations throughout the Sixties, including 'growing hair' dolls, the first Palitoy doll to be advertised on television, and the revolutionary first dressing doll for boys, as well as child-sized doll **Michelle**, 36" tall, that could wear a three-year-old child's own clothes.

By the mid-Sixties British Xylonite had been acquired by the giant General Mills Corp of the USA, and many more mechanical dolls were introduced for the late Sixties and early Seventies, together with American trends in dolls. 1971 saw the formation of a wholesale division called Bradgate to distribute dolls on a vaster scale.

However, by the early Eighties, General Mills had pulled out of the toy business and Hasbro Inc acquired the Palitoy company, ceasing production of the remaining Palitoy dolls by the mid-Eighties. The Coalville factory continues today as Tonka Toys.

Maker: Cascelloid Ltd/Palitoy
Doll name: unknown
Size: 15"/38cm
Marks: 'Palitoy Made in England'
Date: 1960s

Black dolls were made by Palitoy but are very hard to find in hard plastic. This one from the 1960s had a hard vinyl body with soft vinyl head and arms. She has unusual side glancing sleeping eyes and rooted black hair. Fully jointed, she wears her original clothes.

BELOW
Maker: Cascelloid Ltd/Palitoy
Doll name: **Walking Doll**
Size: 15"/38cm
Marks: 'Palitoy Made in England'
Date: 1958

A hard plastic walker with soft vinyl rooted hair in a pony tail style, pictured with her original box. Notice the leaflet shows Paliglide walking dolls **Gillian** and **Sylvia** with sweet closed mouth expressions. (Collection Denise and Tony Slade)

LEFT
Maker: Palitoy
Doll name: **Michelle**
Size: 36"/92cm
Marks: Palitoy
Date: 1961

Child-sized Michelle could wear the clothes of a three-year old.
(Collection Christine Wimsey)

Pedigree Doll & Toys Lines Bros. Ltd

1940s AND 1950s

Three young men, Walter, William and Arthur Lines, made up a 'triangle' of brothers which became their trademark when they left their father's business and started the Lines Bros company in south east London in 1919 after returning from the First World War. They made prams, pedal cars, scooters, rocking horses, dolls houses, clockwork toys etc. When the business was flourishing, they moved to a new, bigger factory at Merton, south west London, in 1924 and registered the Tri-ang (triangle) trademark in 1927. From 1937 the company started to produce a beautiful range of soft toys in many sizes. During the late 1930s they perfected woodflour composition dolls, plaster resin dolls – which were a type of composition, rubber dolls and a range of soft body dolls with composition heads. Their late 1930s catalogue included a superb range of composition dolls, baby, toddler, girl/boy dolls in 10" to 20" sizes, all beautifully dressed. They had painted or metal sleeping eyes and the girls a superior mohair wig in a short Thirties style. Their range of 'Streamline' dolls were slimmer-bodied fashion girls in 13", 15", 17" and 20" sizes, with lovely 1920s- and 1930s-style dresses, coats and hats. The dolls had painted, metal or glass sleeping eyes, jointed limbs and superior mohair wigs. A little range of black, composition baby/toddler dolls was also made with painted eyes, jointed limbs, moulded heads and wearing gingham rompers and dresses.

These composition dolls were marked 'Pedigree Made in England' across a triangle on their backs, or 'Pedigree England' across the back of the neck. The dresses were adorned with a little Pedigree bar brooch with a linked triangle of L. Bros Ltd London England. The name Pedigree was not registered until 1942.

As war loomed, the factory at Merton was requisitioned to make machine guns and munitions for the war effort, employing seven thousand people. In 1946, after the war years, when the factory returned to doll and toy making, hard plastic (cellulose acetate) dolls were soon introduced and large numbers of these dolls have survived, including many from the author's own childhood. Baby dolls, toddlers, girls and boys were all made in hard plastic in many styles, sizes and colours, from flesh, pink, chocolate and black plastic, with glued-on mohair wigs in many styles and colours, including moulded hair for the babies and boys.

Maker: Lines Bros Ltd/Pedigree
Doll name: none
Size: 10"/25.5cm
Marks: 'Pedigree Made in England' across a triangle
Date: late 1930s

A composition baby with strung limbs, moulded hair and painted side-glancing eyes.

◀ PAGE 62
Makers: Pedigree Dolls and Toys/ Lines Bros Ltd
Doll names: **Walker, Negro Baby, Delite**
Sizes: 12"/30.5cm, 10"/25.5cm; 16"/40.5cm
Marks: 'Made in England'; 'Pedigree Made in England'
Dates: 1958, 1953, 1958

The model on the left, a 12" walker was also available in a chocolate brown colour in 1959. The model on the right makes a nice boy but was in fact listed in the catalogue as a girl doll. The 10" negro baby also came with moulded head. All these models are fairly hard to find now.

Maker: Lines Bros Ltd/Pedigree
Doll name: none
Size: 18"/46cm
Marks: 'Pedigree Made in England' across a triangle
Date: late 1930s

Plaster resin composition toddler with moulded hair, painted side-glancing eyes, open closed mouth with two teeth.

Maker: Lines Bros Ltd/Pedigree
Doll name: unknown
Size: 20"/51cm
Marks: 'Pedigree Made in England' across a triangle
Date: late 1930s

Woodflour composition doll with moulded hair, painted side-glancing eyes, open mouth with two teeth. A straight-legged little girl wearing a replica of her original dress, pants and bonnet.

The tiny (Pedigree) bar and (Lines) triangle brooch that was pinned to the original clothing of the doll in above right and all dressed dolls made in the late 1930s.

During the 1950s, Lines Bros acquired many new factories, including ones in South Wales and Northern Ireland, as well as Joy Toys Ltd in New Zealand and factories in Canada, Australia and South Africa, so that Pedigree dolls and toys were available around the world. In 1951 Lines Bros took over Rovex Plastics of Richmond and by 1954 Rovex had moved to Margate, leaving the Richmond factory to be used as an overflow for the Merton factory. A lovely range of dolls' dresses and accessories for fashion-conscious dolls was produced during the late Fifties and early Sixties from the Richmond factory, under the name of Mamselle Boutique. Outfits for girl, boy, baby and teen dolls were made, and even a small range for teddies. The clothes came in a wide range of sizes from 10" to 22", and were made from quality fabrics such as cotton, gingham, pique, seersucker,

Knitting pattern available in the early 1950s for the Pedigree Toddler.

Maker: Pedigree
Doll name: HA Walkie Talkies/Delite Toddler 20"/51cm
Sizes: 21"/53.5cm; 21"/53.5cm; 20"/51cm
Marks: 'Pedigree Made in England' on back of neck in capitals
Date: Late 1940s

A 'family' of dolls with the same face, all have sleeping flirting eyes, closed red lips and rosy cheeks. The girl on the left has a dark brown coarse wig tied in two bunches, is a walking talking doll with ma-ma voice box and grille in her stomach, the boy likewise but with moulded hair. The toddler has moulded hair, bent limbs and a voice box. They have the early walking mechanism, rod from crutch right through to the top of the head with no neck disc, and large hands with seam across the palm. Purchased naked they have been dressed as a family.

Pages from the Mamselle booklet describing some of the wide range of dolls' clothes available in the late 1950s and early 1960s. Depicted are dresses and coats which were available in a wide range of sizes as well as bridal wear for fashion dolls and clothes for teddy bears.

velour, velvet, lace, taffeta, organdie, sailcloth, nylon and acrilan. Some of the first hard plastic dolls made in 1947 were called 'Delite' dolls, and came in various sizes from 6" to 20". Vast quantities were made right through the Fifties, especially in the smaller sizes, dressed in anything from a party dress, school uniform, or famous costumes, or as fairies and story-book characters – the list was endless. Small, naked babies and toddlers were made too, for mother and grandmothers to dress for their offspring. Pedigree made the most of every face mould, making dozens of different variations from each, i.e. bent/straight leg, several different sizes, curved arm/straight arm, three different wig colours, several different wig styles, two eye colours, with or without voice, and dressed in many different outfits. In other words, each doll was mass produced from a mould type and I will endeavour to give examples of many of the doll types made.

Delite Dolls, in 6", 7" and 8" tall were particularly sweet as a baby or little girl or boy. With curved or straight arms and bent or straight legs, black or white flesh plastic, moulded hair or glued on wig dressed in a romper, nappy or floral dress etc. They had sleeping eyes and jointed limbs. Two sets of 6" babies were available from this range: **Little Mother Sewing Set** and **Twins Knitting Set**. From 1955, two more sets were introduced: **Sleepy Head**, a 6" wigged baby

BELOW LEFT
Maker: Lines Bros Ltd/Pedigree
Doll name: **Delite Dolls**
Size: 14"/35.5cm
Marks: 'Pedigree Made in England' across triangle
Date: late 1940s

A moulded hair toddler with sleeping eyes, closed lips and elastic jointed limbs. One of the early hard plastic faces from Pedigree.

BELOW RIGHT
Maker: Lines Bros Ltd/Pedigree
Doll name: **Delite Dolls**
Size: 16"/40cm
Marks: 'Pedigree Made in England' across back of neck
Date: 1948

Made in two sizes: 16" and 20". From the late 1940s through the early 1950s many thousands were made with sleeping flirting eyes, deeply moulded curls and ma-ma voice box with the grille in their backs and elastic strung bodies.

ABOVE
Maker: Lines Bros Ltd/Pedigree
Doll name: **Delite Dolls**
Size: 8"/20cm
Marks: none
Date: early 1950s

The boy illustrated has straight legs and deeply moulded curls. Bent leg versions were also made. All had sleeping eyes and elastic strung limbs. He sits on his original box.

ABOVE RIGHT
Maker: Lines Bros Ltd/Pedigree
Doll name: **Delite Dolls**
Size: 6"/15cm
Marks: none
Date: early 1950s

A sweet rosy-cheeked, bent-leg, suck-thumb baby with moulded hair and sleeping eyes with no lashes. Available also as a straight-leg and with a wig.

RIGHT
Maker: Lines Bros Ltd/Pedigree
Doll name: **Delite Dolls**
Size: 8"/20cm
Marks: none
Date: early 1950s

Bent-leg and straight-leg dolls shown next to an original box.

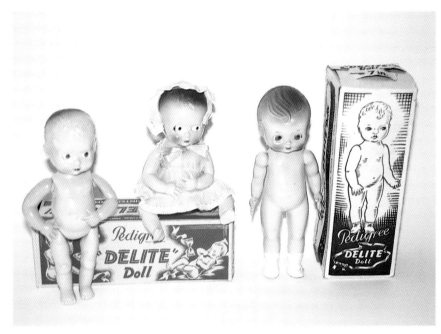

Maker: Lines Bros Ltd/Pedigree
Doll name: **Delite Dolls**
Size: 6"/15cm, 7"/18cm
Marks: none
Date: early 1950s

Straight-leg baby and dressed baby with original box.
On the right a 7" boy with box.
(Collection Denise and Tony Slade)

BELOW LEFT
Maker: Lines Bros Ltd/Pedigree
Doll name: **Delite Dolls**
Size: 6"/15cm
Marks: none
Date: early 1950s

Straight-leg girls undressed and dressed.
The dressed ones came as: blonde wig, blue dress; brunette wig, red dress; honey blonde wig, green dress.

Maker: Lines Bros Ltd/Pedigree
Doll name: **Delite Dolls**
Size: 7"/18cm
Marks: 'Pedigree Made in England' across triangle
Date: early 1950s

Black straight-leg boy with moulded tight curls, sleeping side-glancing eyes and jointed arms.

Maker: Lines Bros Ltd/Pedigree
Doll name: **Delite Dolls**
Size: 7"/18cm
Marks: 'Pedigree Made in England' across triangle
Date: early 1950s

A group of straight-leg Delite dolls showing wigged girl, moulded boy and negro. All have sleeping eyes and jointed arms.

Maker: Lines Bros Ltd/Pedigree
Doll name: **Delite Dolls**
Size: 7"/18cm
Marks: 'Pedigree Made in England' across triangle
Date: early 1950s

Three black Delites, showing moulded-haired boys at each end with wigged girl in centre with an original box.
(Collection Denise and Tony Slade)

Maker: Lines Bros Ltd/Pedigree
Doll name: **Delite Dolls**
Size: 8"/20cm
Marks: 'Made in England' across back
Date: early 1960s

Two attractive Delite girls with mohair wigs, sleeping eyes and straight legs with elastic jointed head and limbs.

Maker: Lines Bros Ltd/Pedigree
Doll name: **Delite Dolls**
Size: 7"/18cm
Marks: 'Pedigree'
Date: early 1950s

Dressed Delites. Left to right: Jack Tar, Bridegroom, Scottish lad and Scottish lass, all standing next to original boxes.
(Collection Denise and Tony Slade)

BELOW LEFT
Maker: Lines Bros Ltd/Pedigree
Doll name: **Delite Dolls**
Size: 10"/25.5cm
Marks: 'Made in England' across back
Date: early 1950s

Black and white babies with astrakhan wig and moulded hair. Both have side-glancing sleeping eyes and elastic strung jointed heads and limbs.

with her own bed, day and night clothes and bed linen; and **Precious Bairn**, a 6" dressed baby with a blanket and Moses basket. The 7" Delites with jointed arms only were dressed costume dolls, including one as a fairy.

Delite Dolls of 10" and 14" tall, came with straight or bent legs, wigged or moulded hair, dressed as boys/girls/babies, and a negro girl and baby in the 14" size. They had sleeping eyes and jointed limbs. This size came also as a **Trousseau Set**, a doll with a change

ABOVE RIGHT
Maker: Lines Bros Ltd/Pedigree
Doll name: **Delite Dolls**
Size: 10"/25.5cm
Marks: 'Pedigree Made in England' across triangle
Date: early 1950s

Four 10" Delites: brunette short hair wig in green dress; blonde short hair wig in blue dress; brunette plaited wig with pink pinny and honey blonde plaited wig in green pinny in original box.
(Collection Denise and Tony Slade)

of clothing, nightie, dressing gown, pants, bonnet and shoes, attractively boxed together, while another variation in this 10" size was a fairy and wand.

Delite Dolls 16" and 20" tall also had the familiar straight or bent legs, were girls/boys/babies with wigs or moulded hair, sleeping eyes and jointed limbs. There were two black dolls in the 16" size, a straight-leg girl with astrakhan wig with candy-stripe or check dress, and a toddler with moulded curls, bent legs and a striped sunsuit.

BELOW LEFT
Maker: Lines Bros Ltd/Pedigree
Doll name: **Delite Dolls**
Size: 10"/25.5cm
Marks: 'Pedigree Made in England' across triangle
Date: mid-1950s

Three straight-leg girls showing different mohair wig colours, brown, black and fair. All have sleeping eyes and fully jointed elastic strung bodies. The centre girl is a chocolate-brown plastic.

BOTTOM LEFT
Maker: Lines Bros Ltd/Pedigree
Doll name: **Delite Dolls**
Size: 10"/25.5cm and 7"/18cm
Marks: 'Pedigree Made in England' and 'Pedigree Made in England' across triangle
Date: early 1950s

On the left a fully jointed 10"/25.5cm fairy with sleeping eyes and carrying a wand. On the right a 7" fairy with straight-legs, jointed arms and sleeping side-glancing eyes. Both have mohair wigs. The fairy on the right was updated with the new face by 1960 and dressed in white and gold.

BOTTOM RIGHT
Maker: Lines Bros Ltd/Pedigree
Doll name: **Delite Dolls**
Size: 16"/40.5cm
Marks: 'Pedigree Made in England'
Date: late 1940s

Girl doll with mohair plaited wig, sleeping flirting blue eyes, strung limbs with ma-ma voice box grille in back. She wears a print dress, underwear, shoes and socks.

ABOVE LEFT
Maker: Lines Bros Ltd/Pedigree
Doll name: **Delite Dolls**
Size: 14"/35.5cm
Marks: 'Pedigree Made in England' across back
Date: early 1950s

Negro bent-leg baby with moulded tight curls, sleeping flirting amber eyes, jointed head and limbs, ma-ma voice box with grille in his back. He wears the original green stripe sunsuit. This doll was also made in a larger size.

ABOVE RIGHT
Maker: Lines Bros Ltd/Pedigree
Doll name: **Delite Negros**
Size: 14"/35.5cm and 16"/40.5cm
Marks: 'Pedigree Made in England'
Date: early 1950s

Group of Negro bent and straight-limbed dolls, two with astrakhan wigs. All have sleeping brown eyes and voice boxes.

All Pedigree **Delite** dolls were also available naked for the child, mother or grandmother to dress, as many knitting and paper dress patterns were available in magazines throughout the Fifties for this favourite pastime, before television viewing filled our lives.

Hand-assisted walking-talking dolls came in three sizes – 12", 16" and 20". The 12" walking dolls had no voice box, sleeping eyes, clenched fists and came in three styles, a moulded-hair boy with a sunsuit and two girls with wigs and dresses, one with short curls, and the other long plaits. In 1953 they had a water-melon type smile, which by the late 1950s had to be changed to a more pouting expression. At that time a chocolate-coloured hard plastic version with two-plaits was also introduced. The 16" walking-talking dolls had attractive faces with open-closed mouth, teeth and a tongue, and sleeping flirting eyes and came with various wigs or moulded head for boys. There was an attractive walking negro girl in this 16" size with astrakhan wig, voice box and a pretty dress. The 20" walking-talking dolls had two different attractive faces with the slightly earlier, late Forties model having a closed mouth, sleeping flirting eyes, a voice

GIRL DOLLS' CLOTHES
To fit 12' & 16' dolls
2 or 3 ozs, 3-ply

WELDONS KNITWEAR 4D A1157

BOY DOLLS' CLOTHES
To fit 12' & 16' dolls
2 or 3 ozs, 3-ply, and contrast

WELDONS KNITWEAR 4D A1156

Maker: Pedigree
Doll name: **Delite Toddler**
Size: 20"/51cm
Marks: 'Pedigree' on back of neck
Date: 1949

One of the author's favourite childhood dolls. A toddler with voice box and grille in stomach, larger type hands with seam across palm. She has moulded hair but has worn an array of glued-on wigs during the early 1950s. Traditional bent legs, open-closed mouth with two teeth and tongue and lovely rosy cheeks. A 'saucy' type. This dress and bonnet becomes her but over the years she has worn many different out-fits, including knitted creations.

Girl and boy doll's clothes patterns purchased in the mid-1950s for 12"/30.5cm to 16"/40.5cm Pedigree dolls.

Maker: Lines Bros Ltd/Pedigree
Doll name: **Hand-Assisted Walker**
Marks: 'Made in England'
Date: 1958

In 1953 these 12" walkers had a water melon smile, which was replaced with a more pouty expression in 1957.

ABOVE MIDDLE
Maker: Lines Bros Ltd/Pedigree
Doll name: **Walking African Girl**
Size: 16"/40.5cm
Marks: 'Pedigree Made in England'
Date: late 1950s

A black-coloured plastic girl with astrakhan wig, hoop earrings, sleeping flirting brown eyes, open-closed mouth with tongue and teeth, jointed limbs, wearing cotton print dress. These black plastic dolls were issued in six sizes: 10"/25.5cm, 12"/30.5cm, 14"/35.5cm, 16"/40.5cm, 20"/51cm and 22"/56cm. Both with moulded curls and curly astrakhan wigs.

ABOVE RIGHT
Maker: Lines Bros Ltd/Pedigree
Doll name: **Walking Asian Girl ('Dusky Dolls')**
Size: 16"/40.5cm
Marks: 'Pedigree Made in England'
Date: late 1950s

A chocolate-coloured plastic girl with black plaited mohair wig, sleeping flirting amber eyes, open-closed mouth with tongue and teeth, jointed walking limbs, wearing a cotton print 'sari-style' dress, underwear, shoes and socks. These 'Dusky' dolls were issued in six sizes as above, all with the two black plaits wig style.

Maker: Pedigree
Doll names: **Mandy Lou, Dixie, Delite Toddler** 20"/51cm
Sizes: (From left to right) 21"/53.5cm, 21"/53.5cm, 20"/51cm
Marks: 'Pedigree England' in signature form on back of neck
Date: 1953

This family of black plastic dolls was made from the same face moulds as the family on page 65. They too had sleeping flirting eyes but all had black astrakhan wigs glued to their heads and accentuated red painted lips. The girl and boy are hand-assisted walkie-talkies with ma-ma voice box and grille in their backs. They have the earlier type hands with seam across palm, but also a neck plate to prevent the head wobbling. The toddler is similar with bent limbs.

box, wigs for girls, and moulded hair for boys, and a bent leg toddler. This model was made in black plastic too, the girl was called **Mandy Lou** and the boy **Dixie**, both having curly astrakhan wigs, together with a bent-leg toddler. Later dolls from 1955 had golden hoop earrings on all three black models. The Fifties face had the open-closed mouth with teeth and a tongue, sleeping flirting eyes, a variety of attractive wigs and a voice box, and were given the name **Saucy Walker**. A bent-leg toddler and chocolate-coloured **Dusky** versions were also made, plus a 'Trousseau' doll called **Felicity** with a travelling case containing hat, coat, dress, pants, socks, shoes, housecoat, nightgown and slippers. New in 1953 were 21" walking dolls and new for 1955 were 22" walking dolls with all the characteristics of the previous 21" series. By 1959 all 16"–22" walking dolls could be supplied with a walking harness at a small extra cost.

In 1953, coronation year, many more dolls were added to the Pedigree range, including **Little Princess**, a 14" straight-legged little girl doll introduced presumably to represent Princess Anne. She was

◀ BELOW RIGHT, PAGE 76
Maker: Lines Bros Ltd/Pedigree
Doll name: **Delite Walking Dolls**
Marks: 'Pedigree Made in England'
Date: late 1940s and early 1950s

A pair of 16" Delite walking talking dolls. Both have sleeping flirting eyes, open closed mouths with tongues and teeth, ma-ma voice boxes with grilles. The girl has a coarse shoulder-length brunette wig and the boy moulded painted hair.

Maker: Pedigree
Doll name: **Saucy Walker 'Dusky' Doll**
Size: 22"/56cm
Marks: 'Pedigree' in signature form on back of neck
Date: mid-1950s, 1955

A 'milk chocolate'-coloured doll with sleeping flirting eyes, dark brown wig in two plaits style, open-closed mouth with two teeth and tongue. She is a hand-assisted walking-talking doll with ma-ma voice box and grille in her back and the newer slimmer hands. She wears a brown gingham school dress typical of the 1950s.

Maker: Lines Bros Ltd/Pedigree
Doll name: **Saucy Walker**
Size: 21"/53.5cm
Marks: 'Pedigree Made in England'
Date: 1953

Walking-talking doll with blonde mohair wig, sleeping-flirting blue eyes, open-closed mouth with tongue and two teeth, wearing a replica of her original dress, underwear, shoes and socks. These dolls were also issued with brunette wigs and other hair styles, including two long plaits.

presented in a regal-looking box decorated with coronets and a picture of a palace. **Little Princess** had sleeping eyes, open-closed mouth with tongue and two teeth, pale blonde short curly wig, and was dressed in nylon underwear, socks, shoes and a taffeta and muslin spotted dress trimmed with lace and ric-rac braid in a choice of several colours: lemon on white, blue on white, green on white and red on white. The dress was designed by Norman Hartnell (dress-maker to the Queen). A pattern depicting other styles for the doll was available for her through *Woman's Illustrated* at that time and included My Coronation Robe, My Long Frock, My Short Frock and My Striped Frock on the one pattern. Another series of patterns included two Balmain Paris frocks, a coat and a suit. There was also a pattern by Sarah Redwood which consisted of a four-way jiffy frock, a play-suit, housecoat and petticoat all on the one pattern for this doll. **Little Princess** dolls and knitting patterns were also available through *Woman's Illustrated* for a while. In 1960 **Little Princess** was reissued as a 15"/38cm vinyl doll. The dress and box for her remained very similar.

BELOW LEFT AND RIGHT
Maker: Lines Bros Ltd/Pedigree
Doll name: **Little Princess**
Size: 14"/35.5cm
Marks: 'Pedigree Made in England'
Date: 1953

Little Princess (presumably named after Princess Anne) was introduced in Coronation year, with pale blonde curly wig, sleeping flirting eyes, rosy cheeks and an open closed mouth with tongue and two teeth. Her dress, designed by Norman Hartnell, was of spotted taffeta, muslin and lace trimmed with ric-rac braid. (Collection Christine Wimsey)

Another Little Princess which has been re-dressed. The original clothes were available in several colours: red spot, blue spot, green spot or lemon spot trimmed with muslin, lace and toning ric-rac braid. Little Princess was re-issued as an all-vinyl doll in 1960 with blonde rooted bubble-cut hair.

ABOVE
Maker: Lines Bros Ltd/Pedigree
Doll name: **Beauty Skin Baby Dolls**
Size: 9"/23cm
Marks: 'Pedigree on back of neck'
Date: 1953

Soft beauty skin hygienically-stuffed body with vinyl moulded head and painted side glancing eyes. Her original clothes have a Pedigree label sewn into them. Later models were issued in an upholstered 'Winkie Crib' with carrying handles.

CENTRE
Maker: Lines Bros Ltd/Pedigree
Doll name: **Beauty Skin**
Size: 14"/36cm
Marks: 'Pedigree Made in England'
Date: 1949

RIGHT
Maker: Lines Bros Ltd/Pedigree
Doll name: **Beauty Skin**
Size: 16"/41cm
Marks: 'Pedigree Made in England'
Date: 1953

Two soft beauty skin dolls with hygienically-stuffed bodies, hard plastic heads and sleeping eyes.
(Right collection Denise and Tony Slade)

Beauty Skin Baby Dolls were introduced in 1949 as it was thought the hard plastic dolls were a little too hard to the touch for younger children. The body and limbs were made of washable latex rubber hygienically stuffed, and the legs were bent. They had hard plastic heads, moulded or wigged, sleeping flirting eyes and a ma-ma voice box. They were made in 16" and 20" sizes. A 10" baby was also made with a soft beauty skin body, hygienically stuffed, fixed limbs and a 'rubbery vinyl' moulded head with painted side glancing eyes. It was recommended that these beauty skin dolls were dusted with talc to keep in fine condition. In 1955 the 10" beauty skin baby was supplied in a plastic 'Winkie Crib', complete with a beautiful baby's layette.

Pin-Up Fashion Dolls and **Teenage Miss Fashion Dolls** were introduced in 1953. These dolls had slimmer bodies, sleeping-flirting eyes and real nylon wigs that could be play-waved and shampooed. The dolls were 'named', the 19" sizes were **Hazel** – fair hair, **Heather** – blonde, and **Beryl** – brunette, all **Pin-Ups**, and **Sylvia** – fair hair and **Janet** – brunette, both **'Teenage Miss'**. The 14" sizes were **Celia** – blonde hair, **Alice** – brunette and **Enid** – fair, all **Pin-Ups** with the **Teenage Miss** styles as **Carol** – brunette, **Sonia** – brunette and **June** – fair, dressed as a bride with two 7" Delite dolls as her attendants, suitably attired as a bridesmaid and page. A fairy with a wand was also made in this 14" size, and for 1953 only a 19" **Pin-Up** attired in

◀ PAGE 81

Makers: Pedigree, Roddy, Rosebud
Doll names: **Pedigree Elizabeth,**
                Roddy Edna,
                Rosebud Chocolate Baby
Sizes: 19"/48.5cm, 17"/46 cm, 13"/33 cm
Marks: None, Pedigree label on dress;
'Roddy Made in Eng'; 'Rosebud Made in
Eng'
Dates: 1953, 1956, 1955

The two girl dolls Elizabeth and Edna are
hard to find in original clothes. The Rosebud baby also came nude for dressing at
home and is slightly easier to find, also in
flesh colour.

These four dressmaking patterns for
Elizabeth show her 'dainty afternoon dress'
which was supplied free with the doll. The
three additional patterns could be
purchased separately from *Woman*
magazine and 'Style' patterns to make a
further twelve outfits for Elizabeth the
Dressmaking Doll.

coronation robes with two 7" Delite dolls as her attendants wearing robes over their usual dresses. Both the **Pin-Up** and Teenage Miss dolls were from the same style mould. However the former wore short dresses, whereas the **Teenage Miss** dolls wore long evening/party-style dresses. The play-wave kit supplied with the **Pin-Up** dolls was by Revlon.

Elizabeth the Dressmaking doll was introduced in 1953 with the same face and body as the **Pin-Up** series, 19" tall and a softer saran nylon wig in a fair colour. She came with pattern D for an afternoon dress. Three further paper patterns containing twelve attractive outfits to make up by *Woman* magazine's fashion designer, Veronica Scott were available for her through the magazine. The fashions consisted of three series: a) beach outfit, suit and blouse, duster coat and night-dress; b) evening dress, evening petticoat, camiknickers and house-coat; c) slip and knickers, winter dress, winter coat and party dress.

LEFT
Maker: Lines Bros Ltd/Pedigree
Doll name: **Pin-Up Fashion Dolls**
Size: 19"/48.5cm
Marks: none
Date: 1953

Two Pin-Up girls wearing replica dresses. They were introduced with Play-Wave sets made by Revlon. The hair could be shampooed and play-waved repeatedly.

RIGHT
Maker: Lines Bros Ltd/Pedigree
Doll name: **Pin-Up Fashion Dolls**
Size: 14"/36cm
Marks: none
Date: 1953

Two smaller Pin-Up girls introduced with Play-Wave sets made by Revlon.

Nurse Nan, also 19" tall, with the same face and body as **Elizabeth** was introduced in 1954 dressed in an authentic nurse's uniform with cape, first aid kit and manual. There was also a 19" series with the same body as **Elizabeth**, but with an open-closed mouth and two teeth and with several different wig styles including two long plaits. By 1959 these 19" teen body dolls were issued with Tender-Tex vinyl rooted hair heads.

Maker: Lines Bros Ltd/Pedigree
Doll name: **Elizabeth**
Size: 19"/48.5cm
Marks: none
Date: 1953

This illustration of Elizabeth shows her wearing a two-piece suit and blouse made from the pattern A pictured beside her. Other designs on pattern A were beach outfit, duster coat and nightdress. On pattern B were evening dress and waist petticoat, camiknickers and housecoat. On pattern C, slip and knickers, winter dress, winter coat and party dress.

Maker: Lines Bros Ltd/Pedigree
Doll name: **Elizabeth**
Size: 19"/48.5cm
Marks: none
Date: 1953

Elizabeth the Dressmaking Doll is wearing her original clothes designed by Veronica Scott of *Woman* magazine. She had a fair mohair wig that could be brushed and combed, sleeping flirting eyes and a slimmer jointed 'teenage' body.

Maker: Lines Bros Ltd/Pedigree
Doll name: **Elizabeth**
Size: 19"/48.5cm
Marks: none
Date: 1953

Seen here, another Elizabeth wearing her two-piece suit and standing next to her original box.
(Collection Christine Wimsey)

Magic Flesh dolls were also introduced in 1953 with a vinyl skin-like one-piece body, arms and legs, rooted hair vinyl heads or vinyl moulded heads. They included **Angela**, a 20" bent-leg toddler, **Kate**, for one year only an 18", a 16" straight-leg girl, plus 10" babies, one with a trousseau. By 1955 another 20" baby doll in this range was called **Cherub**, with rooted curly hair and a presentation box with day and night clothes and toilet accessories.

Maker: Lines Bros Ltd/Pedigree
Doll name: **Nurse Nan**
Size: 19"/48.5cm
Marks: none
Date: 1955

Nurse Nan was made for five years. She came dressed in an authentic nurse's uniform with a cape, first aid kit and manual.

Maker: Lines Bros Ltd/Pedigree
Doll name: 19" **Delite** series
Size: 19"/48.5cm
Marks: none
Date: 1955/6

This series had several wig styles and colours, plus several plaid and checked dress styles. Made from the same body mould as Elizabeth and the Pin-Up series.

Clockwork Toddling Dolls. From 1953 these 8" and 14" dolls had a clockwork winding mechanism – key in the back – that enabled them to toddle along like many clockwork toys of the day. They had rather large feet to keep them balanced. Two versions were made in the 14" size, a boy with moulded hair in a romper suit and a wigged girl in a dress. In the 8" size, a little series of male characters was made: Toddler Boy, Jock the Highland Lad, Steve the Jockey, Jazzy the Conductor, Monty Man About Town, Joey the Clown.

Maker: Lines Bros Ltd/Pedigree
Doll name: **Clockwork Dolls**
Size: 14"/35.5cm
Marks: 'Pedigree Made in England'
Date: 1953

This clockwork doll was made as a moulded-hair boy or wigged girl (illustrated here) in 14"/35.5cm and 8"/20cm as little characters. She has a coarse nylon brunette wig, sleeping flirting eyes, open-closed mouth with tongue and two teeth and a wind-up clockwork walking mechanism with key in her back. When she is wound up she toddles along on her large feet, with painted shoes and socks. This one has toddled off the table a few times and has been repaired.

Maker: Lines Bros Ltd/Pedigree
Doll name: **Clockwork Dolls**
Size: 14"/35.5cm
Marks: 'Pedigree Made in England'
Date: 1953

Clockwork doll with moulded hair, sleeping flirting eyes, open closed mouth with teeth and wind-up clockwork mechanism. When wound the doll toddles along.
(Collection Christine Wimsey)

Playfella Dolls, 17" tall, had plastic heads and hands with soft body and limbs. Dressed as cowboys, 'indians', sailor etc, they were also available from 1954.

In 1955 two larger dolls were introduced to the range and were both hand-assisted walking-talking dolls.

LEFT
Maker: Lines Bros Ltd/Pedigree
Doll name: **Pretty Peepers**
Size: 22"/56cm
Marks: 'Pedigree Made in England'
Date: 1957/9

A blonde-wigged Pretty Peepers wearing a red pinafore.

Knee Jointed Dolls, 1955, and **Pretty Peepers**, 1957–59. These were 22" dolls with short curly, or two plaits-style wigs in blonde or brunette, sleeping flirting eyes and knee-joints enabling the doll to kneel and sit naturally. The knee-joint series had a voice box and were dressed in attractive cotton dresses, underwear, socks and shoes. In 1958 a range of 12" knee-joint dolls was introduced with vinyl-rooted heads for just one year. By 1960 they were replaced by 10" **Miss Suzette**, a hard plastic teen type doll with jointed knees, arched feet and a rayon wig. She came boxed, wearing camiknickers,

Maker: Lines Bros Ltd/Pedigree
Doll name: **Pretty Peepers**
Size: 22"/56cm
Marks: 'Pedigree Made in England'
Date: 1957/9

A brunette-wigged Pretty Peepers wearing a yellow pinafore.
(Collection Christine Wimsey)

Maker: Pedigree
Doll name: **Knee Jointed Walker**
Size: 22"/56cm
Marks: 'Pedigree' in signature style on back of neck, 'Made in England' across shoulders
Date: 1955

Lovely knee-jointed hand-assisted walkie-talkie dolls showing two wig colours. They had sleeping flirting eyes, open-closed mouths with tongue and two teeth. The grille for the ma-ma voice box appears on their backs. With Pretty Peepers the voice box is omitted and replaced with a roller mechanism activated from a chest plate in the front of the doll's body. The dolls can kneel and sit very naturally as the illustration shows. They were supplied in assorted cotton print dresses of which these two are replicas. The small doll is a Pedigree 8"/20cm Delite with plaited wig made in the late 1950s.

The naked body of a knee-jointed hand-assisted walking-talking doll. Virtually the same as a conventional walker except the thigh to knee is on a sprung rod enabling the lower leg to be pulled down into a sitting position. These dolls had the post-1952 slimmer body shape.

shoes and nylon stockings. Her range of six dresses was boxed and sold separately. She too was discontinued after only one year. Whereas **Pretty Peepers** was made for almost three years from 1957, and had the same knee-joints, her voice box was replaced with a roller mechanism in the head activated from a chest plate that, when depressed, changed the colour of the eyes from blue to brown. The sequence went from flirting left then right, before looking forward and changing from blue to brown, and repeating over again each time the plate was pressed. The Pedigree catalogue stated that **Pretty Peepers** is 'The most accomplished doll in the world! **Pretty Peepers** is so versatile that no little girl can ever tire of her, she has such endless possibilities as a playtime companion. No other doll can equal her! She can walk dance and sit down, her eyes look from left to right, they change from blue to brown and close'. These knee-jointed dolls are now quite difficult to find, presumably due to the short time they were in production and the number of breakable parts.

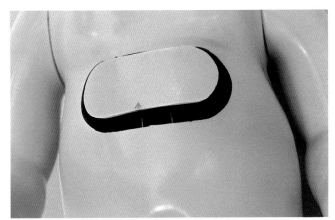

Chest plate for Pretty Peepers. This replaced the ma-ma voice box and enabled the eyes to change position and colour when depressed.

Maker: Lines Bros Ltd/Pedigree
Doll name: **Knee Joint Dolls**
Size: 12"/31cm
Marks: 'Pedigree Made in England'
Date: 1958

This knee-joint series was made for one year only. The two on the left are hard plastic with blonde and brunette wigs respectively and the doll on the right has a rooted fair-haired vinyl head on a jointed-knee, hard plastic body.
(Collection Denise and Tony Slade)

Maker: Pedigree
Doll name: **Belles of Brighton**
Size: 28"/71cm
Marks: 'Pedigree' in signature style on back of neck, 'Made in England' across shoulders
Date: 1955

These very tall hand-assisted walking-talking dolls came with blonde curly wigs or brunette plaits. They had sleeping-flirting eyes, open mouths with tongue and four teeth, ma-ma voice box with the grille in the back of the body. They were supplied in assorted dresses and Pedigree marked shoes.

Belles of Brighton. 26" and 28" walking-talking dolls with two wig styles, blonde curly or long brunette plaits, with sleeping-flirting eyes, dresses, underclothes, shoes and socks. By 1963 these dolls had vinyl-rooted heads.

Pedigree hard plastic dolls are usually marked on the back of the neck or across the shoulders either in capitals or the familiar signature. Earlier dolls, pre-1950 moulds and the small Delite dolls had the Pedigree signature across the Lines Bros triangle.

Pedigree introduced **Tender Tex** all-vinyl baby, girl and boy dolls in 1957, but continued into the Sixties with a few hard plastic dolls in the form of the 7" **Delite** characters and costume dolls with an updated face. 8" Delite girls were issued as '**Carry me Case**' dolls in three different coloured carry-cases complete with two outfits of clothing, and **Highland Dolls** came in 7" to 16" sizes, dressed in a variety of authentic tartans – Royal Stewart, Dress Stewart, Buchanan, MacBeth, Napier, MacLeod, Anderson, Princess Elizabeth, Ross, MacDonald, MacGregor, Cameron and Gordon. Large child-sized vinyl dolls were introduced in 1960, able to wear a three-year-old child's clothes, with names like **Shirley, Mary-Ann, Melanie** and **Jennifer**. Vinyl-rooted hair heads on hard plastic bodies were introduced too, but by 1964 most of the hard plastic dolls had been phased out in favour of the all-vinyl doll ranges. That year also saw the company renamed Pedigree Dolls Ltd, while the early Sixties saw the introduction of **Sindy** and friends, 12" vinyl teen fashion dolls.

By 1968 Rovex Industries had taken over the running of Pedigree Dolls with a move to new premises in Canterbury by 1969. In 1972 the company was taken over by the American firm Dunbee Combex Marx, part of the General Mills Group. By 1980 General Mills had pulled out of the toy market and the company was run by Tamwade Ltd under a management buyout which ceased trading in 1986. At this point Sindy was sold to Hasbro UK and Pedigree to Rodston, now used under licence by Spearhead Industries.

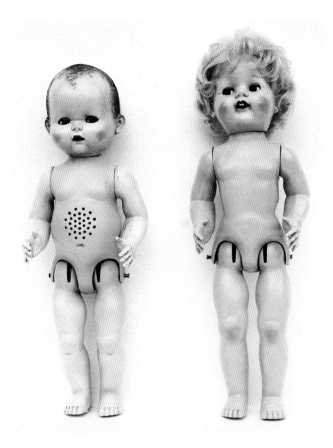
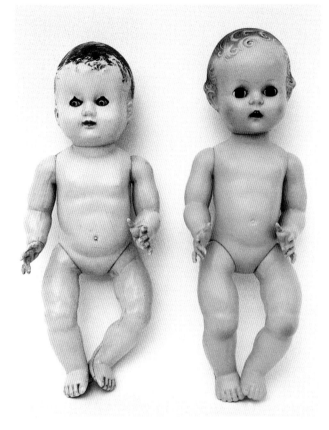

ABOVE LEFT

This illustration shows the two body types of the hand-assisted walking-talking Pedigree dolls. On the left, a pre-1952 doll with plump body, sealed ma-ma voice box with grille on stomach. Wobbly head as metal rod runs from the crutch to the top of the head with no neck disc. Large hands with seam across palm. On the right, post-1952 with slimmer body, replaceable ma-ma voice box with removable grille in back. The metal rod from the crutch to the top of the head passes through a neck disc which prevents wobble. The hands are smaller with no seam across the palm. All the pins which hold the Pedigree doll legs in position have unpainted screwheads as shown here.

ABOVE RIGHT

The pre-1952 baby doll at left has the plump body and usually a removable voice box. The baby on the right has the slimmer body and replaceable voice box.

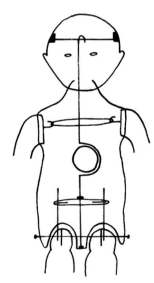

Diagram of an early body showing the rods that assist the walking movement, and the ma-ma voice box in the centre of the body. The arms are strung separately.

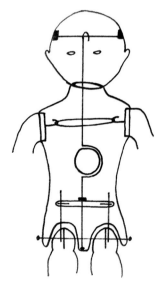

This diagram shows the post-1952 body which is slimmer and has a neck disc and replaceable voice box, with grille in doll's back.

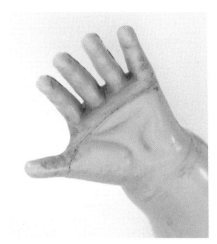

This hand from a 1950 doll shows a larger palm with a seam line across it.

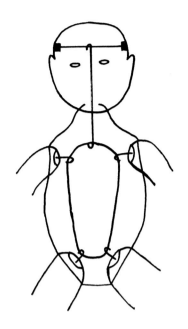

This diagram shows how a toddler boy is elastic strung. The method is virtually the same for all baby dolls.

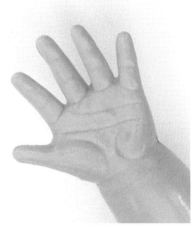

This hand from a post-1952 doll has a smaller palm with no seam line.

The mark: 'Pedigree Made in England' across a Lines Triangle appears on pre-1950 dolls with the exception of the 7" Delites whose moulds were used into the 1960s.

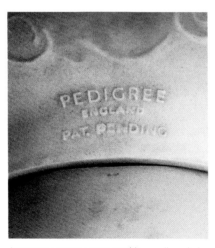

'PEDIGREE MADE IN ENGLAND' in small capitals was used on dolls around 1948 to 1952.

'Pedigree' in signature form plus 'Made in England' underneath was used from about 1953 onwards.

NOTE: These clues can only be used as a rough guide to dating a doll as 'factory put-togethers' and 'unmarked dolls' often turn up and make nonsense of all attempts to accurately date a doll.

Maker: Lines Bros Ltd/Pedigree
Doll name: Carry Me Case Dolls
Size: 8"/20cm
Marks: 'Made in England' on doll, 'Pedigree' on case
Date: 1960

Similar to the cardboard boxed 'Trousseau' dolls of the early 1950s, these 8" Delite dolls were fully jointed with sleeping eyes and mohair wigs. The carry case is plastic-covered cardboard and contains the doll, a nightie, dressing gown, day dress and pants with hat and shoes. When the case is closed, the doll looks out through the window. This case and accessories are in red and white.

Maker: Lines Bros Ltd/Pedigree
Doll name: Carry Me Case Dolls
Size: 8"/20cm
Marks: 'Made in England' on doll, 'Pedigree' on case
Date: 1960

Blonde-wigged doll in a cream carry case. The doll on the left is from the same mould but with bent legs.

Identical to the set shown above with a blonde-wigged, hard plastic Delite doll in a blue case with blue and white clothes and accessories.

Maker: Lines Bros Ltd/Pedigree
Doll name: **Delite Character Dolls**
Size: 7"/18cm
Marks: 'Made in England'
Date: early 1960s

These updated 7" Delites were issued in the early 1960s as 'Character Dolls' and 'Period Miniatures' in both 7"/18cm and 13"/33cm sizes with moulded hair for boys and wigs for girls. Many of the original 1950s outfits were also reissued. This illustration shows two little girls on the left with brunette wigs and one with an auburn wig on the right. They have one-piece bodies, jointed arms and sleeping eyes with lashes.

ABOVE RIGHT
Maker: Lines Bros Ltd/Pedigree
Doll name: **Highland Dolls: Bonnie Charlie and Highland Girl**
Size: 14"/35.5cm
Marks: 'Pedigree Made in England'
Date: 1955

14" straight and bent-leg dolls with deeply moulded hair, dressed in authentic Scottish tartans. They have sleeping eyes, open closed mouths with tongue and teeth, jointed limbs with ma-ma voice box with grille in the back. These dolls were reissued in 1957 wearing a black jacket and hat. The girl has been re-dressed. A wide range of Highland dolls was available in 1959, in several doll sizes and styles.

◀ BELOW RIGHT PAGE 94
Maker: Lines Bros Ltd/Pedigree
Doll name: **Delite Character Dolls**
Size: 7"/18cm
Marks: 'Made in England'
Date: early 1960s

Two more Delite Characters: on the left, chocolate-coloured plastic with black wig and brown sleeping eyes, and on the right, black plastic, moulded hair and original clothes called 'Rastus'.

RIGHT
Maker: Pedigree Dolls and Toys
Doll name: **Walker**
Size: 21"/61cm
Marks: Made in England
Date: 1960

Hard plastic body with a rooted-hair vinyl head.

ABOVE RIGHT
Maker: Lines Bros Ltd/Pedigree
Doll name: unknown
Size: 21"/61cm
Marks: Made in England
Date: late 1950s

This doll has the late '40s plump hard plastic body with ma-ma voice box and grille on stomach. Large hands with seam across palm, but a soft vinyl-rooted hair head with neck disc, closed lips and sleeping eyes. Obviously the factory was using up the older style bodies with this range of new vinyl heads! The doll was purchased like this in the late 1950s.

LEFT
Maker: Lines Bros Ltd/Pedigree
Doll name: **Jennifer**
Size: 35"/89cm
Marks: none on doll; Pedigree brooch on dress
Date: early 1960s

Child-size dolls were the fashion of the early 1960s with most doll manufacturers making them. This one is heavy and made of hard vinyl with rooted blonde hair and sleeping eyes. She is dressed in taffeta and flock-sprayed nylon, ribbon trimmed, with a Pedigree signature golden brooch pinned to the skirt of her dress. These brooches continued to be used by Pedigree throughout the '60s and '70s as many of the dolls themselves were no longer marked. Other versions of this large doll were Shirley, another blonde, Mary-Ann, and Melanie, two brunettes. The teddy bear was also made by Pedigree in the '60s.

Maker: Lines Bros Ltd/Pedigree
Doll name: **Little Gretel**
Size: 8"/20cm
Marks: 'Made in England'
Date: 1960

Blonde plaited Delite with Copley knitting
set and pattern for a child to knit an outfit
for her doll.

Maker: Lines Bros Ltd/Pedigree
Doll name: **Susan**
Size: 13"/33cm
Marks: 'Made in England' across back;
'Pedigree Susan' on box
Date: late 1950s

Hard plastic body with rooted-vinyl head.
Hair is tied in a ponytail and she has
sleeping eyes and a fully-jointed elastic-
strung body.
(Collection Christine Wimsey)

Roddy/ *D. G. Todd & Co Ltd*

1938 TO 1969

Toy Time Toys Ltd in Southport was the beginning of the Roddy doll company. Mr D.G. Todd started in the toy business in the Thirties with this small company making composition dolls and a range of pottery-headed, hard- and cloth-bodied dolls including negros, which were largely unmarked.

Mr Todd and his partner Mr Robinson subsequently formed another company, D.G. Todd & Co Ltd to market a range of an early type of plastic dolls. The dolls used a pale hard shiny plastic with painted tin sleeping eyes and were marked 'Rodnoid Made in England' on their backs. The range of 3" to 9" babies had moulded hair and some a little swatch of mohair on the head. Head and body were in one piece, joined down the sides in two halves, with strung arms and legs. The company did not use Rodnoid as their trademark for long, as it resembled another, and instead registered the name Roddy – a derivation of Robinson and Todd – in 1948. Composition dolls continued after the war in several sizes with sleeping eyes, mohair wigs and strung limbs, many being designed by Mabel Lucie Attwell, a London artist and doll designer working for several companies in the Twenties, Thirties and Forties. These composition dolls were unmarked and are difficult to identify today without the box.

LEFT
Maker: D.G. Todd & Co Ltd/Roddy
Doll name: none
Size: 9"/23cm
Marks: 'Rodnoid Made in England' across the back
Date: 1940s

A pale, hard shiny plastic, one-piece-bodied doll with jointed limbs, sleeping painted tin eyes and moulded hair.
(Collection Christine Wimsey)

RIGHT
Maker: D.G. Todd & Co Ltd/Roddy
Doll name: unknown
Size: 9"/23cm
Marks: 'Made in England'
Date: 1940s

Another pale, hard shiny plastic doll with a one-piece body and jointed limbs. She has sleeping painted tin eyes and a little swatch of pale yellow hair. Her 3"/7.5cm dollie is marked Roddy and also has painted tin sleeping eyes and jointed arms.

Maker: Roddy/D. G. Todd & Co Ltd
Doll names: **Girl, Baby, Walker**
Sizes: 10"/25.5cm, 9"/23cm, 12"/30.5cm
Marks: 'Roddy Made in England'
Date: 1950s

Three different Roddy faces popular
throughout the 1950s.

The more typical hard plastic dolls with a duller finish were made in 1948, and at first 3" and 6" dolls were made with a one-piece straight-legged body, jointed arms with clenched fists and a separate thumb, painted tin sleeping eyes and moulded hair, that could be dressed as a boy or girl. 6" and 9" baby dolls soon followed and had moulded hair for boys or a little swatch of mohair glued on for girls. They had the same, by now familiar, clenched fist with separate thumb and unusual shaped feet. By 1950 a 12" walking doll was added to the range with the same clenched fists, pursed lips and moulded-on shoes. These dolls turned their heads from side to side in an ungainly way as they walked because the metal rod was fixed from the crutch right through to the top of the head without a disc controlling the movement at the neck as in larger dolls of this type. A version who could be made to nod for 'yes' and shake its head for 'no' by pushing buttons on the stomach and back came out in 1950.

During the early Fifties Roddy dolls had three different faces – a 'pouty' face, a smiling face with two teeth and a tongue, and a serious face. All three face-types were made in 13", 16" and 22" sizes including black plastic, both in a straight-leg walkie- talkie version and bent-leg toddler versions, many with voice boxes, moulded hair for boys and attractive wigs in various styles and colours for girls. These

Maker: D.G. Todd & Co Ltd/Roddy
Doll name: unknown
Size: 15"/38cm
Marks: none
Date: late 1940s

A lovely composition doll designed by Mabel Lucy Atwell for Roddy, with a pale blonde mohair wig, sleeping eyes, open-closed mouth and a jointed strung body. Her box too was also designed by the famous doll artist. The doll is all original. (Collection Christine Wimsey)

Maker: D.G. Todd & Co Ltd/Roddy
Doll name: unknown
Size: 3"/7.5cm and 6"/15cm
Marks: 'Roddy Made in England'
Date: late 1940s/1950s

These one-piece-body dolls were first made in the late 1940s. The first ones were pale with painted tin eyes like the 3"/7.5cm babies and 6"/15cm boy on the left. The girl is later with glassene eyes and a mohair wig. All have elastic-strung arms. Both the 3" and 6" sizes were also available in black plastic.

Maker: D.G. Todd & Co Ltd/Roddy
Doll name: none
Size: 3"/7.5cm
Marks: 'Roddy Made in England'
Date: late 1940s/1950s

On either end, white flesh-coloured dolls
and in the centre a black doll.
(Collection Denise and Tony Slade)

Maker: D.G. Todd & Co Ltd/Roddy
Doll name: none
Size: 9"/23cm, 7"/18cm
Date: late 1940s

Two babies with painted tin eyes of shiny
hard plastic. Their boxes state 'Plastic doll
with sleeping eyes and movable limbs'.
(Collection Denise and Tony Slade)

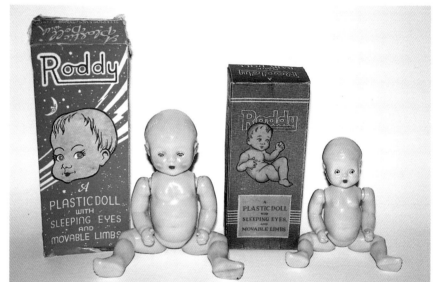

Maker: D.G. Todd & Co Ltd/Roddy
Doll name: none
Size: 7"/18cm walker and 6"/15cm straight
legs
Date: late 1940s

The 7" walker on the left with its box was
also made as a 9" walker. The other three
dolls are black, flesh and chocolate-
coloured 6" straight-leg dolls with sleeping
eyes.
(Collection Denise and Tony Slade)

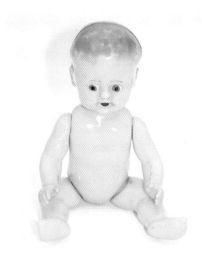

Maker: D.G. Todd & Co Ltd/Roddy

Maker: D.G. Todd & Co Ltd/Roddy
Doll name: none
Size: 8"/20cm
Marks: 'Roddy Made in England'
Date: early 1950s

A little 'Top knot' black baby with three
black mohair top knots tied with ribbon on
a moulded head. Hoop earrings, a one-
piece head and body and jointed limbs. She
was originally boxed with a 3"/12.5cm
black baby but now poses with a white
Roddy baby.

Maker: D.G. Todd & Co Ltd/Roddy
Doll name: none
Size: 8"/20cm
Marks: 'Roddy Made in England'
Date: early 1950s

Black 'top knot' baby pictured with a
3"/8cm black standing baby.
(Collection Denise and Tony Slade)

Maker: D.G. Todd & Co Ltd/Roddy
Doll name: **Walker**
Size: 12"/30.5cm
Marks: 'Roddy Made in England'
Date: 1950

These little 'pouty'-faced walkers were
introduced around 1950 and produced for
several years. They have a wobbly head,
walking mechanism, mohair wigs on girls
and moulded hair on boys, sleeping eyes
and jointed arms, with the familiar clenched
fists and upward pointing thumbs. Many
have painted shoes. This one has her
original clothes. This model was also
available as a black plastic doll.

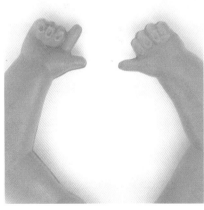

A close-up of the clenched fists with
upward pointing thumbs on all small hard
plastic Roddy dolls. The Pedigree 12"
walker also had these thumbs but a
different face.

dolls were made until the early sixties. Slimmer-bodied, 5" to 11" teen-style dolls with sleeping eyes were made in hard plastic with moulded black shoes for use as costume dolls and silver shoes for fairies and ballerinas. Some had straight legs and jointed arms and were used as costume dolls, while the larger ones, called **Walking Princess**, were walkie dolls with various wig styles and colours including plaits. Patterns for eight outfits were available. A few small novelty dolls were made too, including 4" walking toddlers and 6"

Maker: D.G. Todd & Co Ltd/Roddy
Doll name: none
Size: 11"/28cm
Marks: 'Roddy Made in England'
Date: 1950s

A 'smiling'-faced straight-leg girl with blonde mohair wig, sleeping eyes with no lashes, open closed mouth with tongue and two teeth. She has elastic-strung jointed head and limbs.

Maker: D.G. Todd & Co Ltd/Roddy
Doll name: none
Size: 11"/28cm
Marks: 'Roddy Made in England'
Date: 1950s

A lovely brunette-wigged version of the bent-legged 'smiling'-faced little girl on page 98. She has sleeping eyes with lashes, open closed mouth with teeth and tongue and elastic-strung head and limbs. She sits in her original clothes next to her box.
(Collection Christine Wimsey)

little girls with moulded-on clothes and shoes in various attractive colours. The arms were jointed from beneath the puffed sleeves of the dress. The toddlers had moulded-on rompers and needed a sloping surface to toddle down.

Knee Bend Dolls were made by the company too, including the smiling faced, 13", hard plastic dolls with vinyl rooted heads in 1955. The dolls had jointed knees, arms and legs and could kneel and sit in natural positions.

Maker: D.G. Todd & Co Ltd/Roddy
Doll name: **Walker**
Size: 21"/53cm
Marks: 'Roddy Made in England'
Date: 1950s

Smiling-faced walker with brunette plaits and original dress of nylon taffeta.

Maker: D.G. Todd & Co Ltd/Roddy
Doll name: none
Size: 11"/28cm
Marks: 'Roddy Made in England'
Date: 1950s

A moulded hair, bent leg, 'smiling'-faced boy with sleeping eyes, no lashes, open-closed mouth with a tongue and two teeth. He too has an elastic strung-jointed head and limbs.

Maker: Roddy
Doll name: **Walking Talking Doll**
Size: 22"/56cm
Marks: 'Roddy Made in England' in signature form across shoulders
Date: mid-1950s

A 'serious'-faced Roddy girl walkie-talkie with ma-ma voice box and grille in her back. She has blue sleeping eyes and a glued-on mohair wig which has had the curl trimmed off. These dolls were made in three sizes, and this one has been re-dressed in a schoolgirl-style frock so reminiscent of the '50s.

Maker: Roddy
Doll name: **Walking Talking Doll**
Size: 22"/56cm
Marks: 'Roddy Made in England' in signature form on back of neck
Date: 1955

This is the Roddy 'pouty' face. These dolls were made in three sizes with or without wigs. A hand-assisted walking-talking doll with a grille in her back. They had very plump bodies and chunky limbs, sleeping eyes and rosy cheeks. She wears her original shoes marked Roddy and a replica of an early 1950s' dress.

Maker: Roddy
Doll name: **Walking Talking Doll**
Size: 22"/56cm
Marks: 'Roddy Made in England' in signature form on back of neck
Date: 1955

This black plastic doll is identical to that at left, except for her colour and black glued-on mohair wig and amber sleeping eyes.

ABOVE LEFT
Maker: D.G. Todd & Co Ltd/Roddy
Doll name: none
Size: 10"/25.5cm
Marks: 'Roddy Made in England Pats
Pending'
Date: 1950s

Black bent-limb baby with moulded hair,
amber sleeping eyes and a 'pouty' face with
jointed head and limbs. He too has the
clenched fists with upward pointing thumbs.

ABOVE RIGHT
Maker: D.G. Todd & Co Ltd/Roddy
Doll names: **Walkers**
Size: 15"/38cm
Marks: 'Roddy Made in England'
Date: 1950s

Two black Roddy walking girls with pouty
faces: on the left with black saran wig; on
the right with black astrakhan wig and hoop
earrings.
(Collection Denise and Tony Slade)

Maker: D.G. Todd & Co Ltd/Roddy
Doll names: none
Size: 11"/28cm, 12"/31cm
Marks: 'Roddy Made in England'
Date: 1950s

Two black Roddy babies with moulded hair
and pouty faces.
(Collection Denise and Tony Slade)

ABOVE LEFT
Maker: Roddy
Doll name: unknown
Size: 22"/56cm
Marks: 'Roddy Made in England' in signature form across shoulders
Date: mid-1950s

A lovely chunky toddler with the 'smiling' face, sleeping eyes, open-closed mouth with two teeth and a tongue. He has a ma-ma voice box with grille in his stomach, moulded hair and unusually smooth feet. This doll could be dressed as a girl or boy and this one wears a romper with a tiny animal print.

ABOVE RIGHT
Maker: D.G. Todd & Co Ltd/Roddy
Doll name: unknown
Size: 22"/56cm
Marks: 'Roddy Made in England'
Date: early 1950s

A 'pouty' faced toddler with moulded hair and sleeping eyes. His plump body had elastic-strung bent limbs and unusual smooth feet, as well as a ma-ma voice box with grille in his back.

Maker: D.G. Todd & Co Ltd/Roddy
Doll names: unknown
Size: 22"/56cm, 13"/33cm, 22"/56cm
Marks: 'Roddy Made in England'
Date: 1950s

Three 'pouty'-faced Roddys showing the bent-leg toddlers and straight-leg walkies in the various sizes made.

ABOVE LEFT

Maker: D.G. Todd & Co Ltd/Roddy
Doll name: none
Size: 7"/18cm
Marks: 'Roddy Made in England'
Date: 1950s

These 7" Roddys were made as costume dolls and had straight legs, jointed arms, mohair wigs and sleeping eyes without lashes. These two have been dressed as teenagers.

ABOVE RIGHT

Maker: D.G. Todd & Co Ltd/Roddy
Doll names: **Walker**
Size: 11"/28cm
Marks: 'Roddy Made in England'
Date: 1950s

Roddy costume doll and slim black walker.

Maker: D.G. Todd & Co Ltd/Roddy
Doll name: **Walker**
Size: 6"/15cm
Marks: 'Roddy Made in England'
Date: 1950

These tiny walkers with moulded-on clothes came in pink, blue, red and white dresses.

ABOVE
Maker: D.G. Todd & Co Ltd/Roddy
Doll name: **Walking Doll**
Size: 13"/33cm
Marks: 'Roddy Made in England'
Date: early 1950s

Walking girls like this have the 'smiling' face with sleeping eyes, rosy cheeks and a brunette mohair wig. They also have an unusual neck action: as they walk, the rod from the crutch to the top of the head swings the head from side to side, as it has no neck plate to control it. These dolls have separate elastic-strung arms.

ABOVE CENTRE
Maker: D.G. Todd & Co Ltd/Roddy
Doll name: **Walking Doll**
Size: 13"/33cm
Marks: 'Roddy Made in England'
Date: 1950s

A 'serious'-faced walking girl with sleeping eyes, auburn mohair wig, slimmer body with walking mechanism within the body giving a smooth external finish. Elastic-strung arms.

ABOVE RIGHT
Maker: D.G. Todd & Co Ltd/Roddy
Doll name: **Walking Doll**
Size: 16"/40.5cm
Marks: 'Roddy Made in England'
Date: 1950s

A 16" 'serious'-faced walker with sleeping eyes, brunette mohair wig, walking mechanism inside body leaving a smooth body, and jointed strung arms.

RIGHT
Maker: D.G. Todd & Co Ltd/Roddy
Doll name: **Walking Doll**
Size: 16"/40.5cm
Marks: Roddy Made in England
Date: 1950s

Another 'smiling'-faced walking doll, this time 16" tall, wearing her original clothes and standing in front of her box. Her swing ticket says 'Walking doll from Roddy – made in England', and on the reverse, 'She walks – she sits – she sleeps'.
(Collection Christine Wimsey)

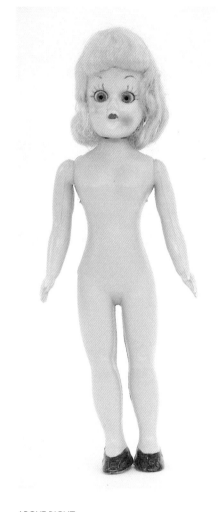

ABOVE LEFT
Maker: D.G. Todd & Co Ltd/Roddy
Doll name: unknown
Size: 11"/28cm
Marks: 'Roddy Made in England'
Date: 1950s

A larger teen-style doll with silver shoes, she was probably dressed as a fairy. Her walking mechanism is internal, she has strung arms, a glued-on mohair wig and sleeping eyes.

ABOVE CENTRE
The body of a 'hidden mechanism' walking doll. Her head turns as she walks and her legs protrude slightly at the hips but the body is completely smooth, with no rod or screw heads showing.

ABOVE RIGHT
Naked Roddy 7", showing straight legs, jointed arms and painted shoes.

LEFT
Maker: D.G. Todd & Co Ltd/Roddy
Doll names: **Edna**
Size: 17"/46cm
Marks: 'Roddy Made in England'
Date: 1956

Edna came with a brunette, auburn or blonde wig in neat curled style and several joints at neck, shoulders, elbows, wrists, waist, legs and knees.
(Collection Alice Brooker)

Roddy hard plastic dolls were marked on their backs in signature form 'Roddy made in England', and are easily recognisable by this or from their distinctive faces, or the clenched fists with separate thumbs on the smaller dolls. By the mid-Fifties the hard plastic heads on the sad-faced dolls were replaced with vinyl Roddy dolls, including teenage twist-waist dolls with eye makeup, arched feet with high-heeled sandals, lingerie and stockings, rooted hair and earrings. These dolls were 15" tall and marked the company's entry into the vinyl era. Many lovely vinyl dolls were made in the early Sixties, including a large girl dressed as a bride and **Choosy Susi**, to name but two. In 1965 the company was sold and the name changed in 1969 to Bluebell Dolls. By 1974 they had come under the umbrella of the General Mills Group and doll production ceased.

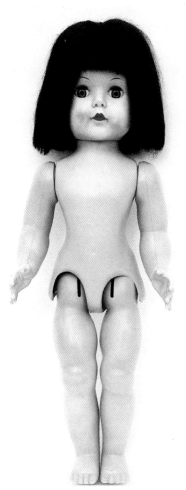

The body of a conventional Roddy Walking Doll. The pin-joint screw head holding the legs in place does not protrude through the plastic at the hips as in Pedigree dolls. The arms are elastic-strung.

Naked body of a Roddy elastic-strung baby doll.

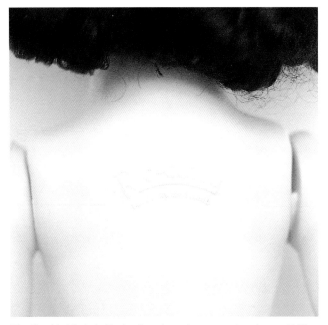

The 'Roddy Made in England' trademark appeared on larger 1950s hard plastic dolls.

The Roddy trademark that appears on smaller baby dolls.

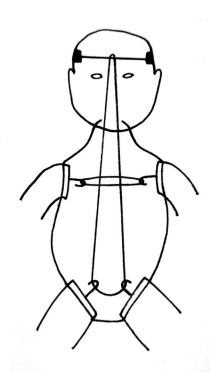

Rough sketch of body stringing on Roddy baby/toddler dolls.

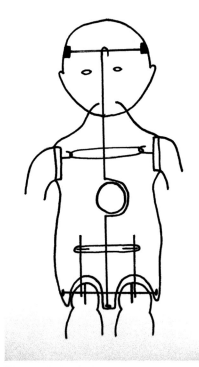

This rough sketch shows the conventional Roddy walking mechanism with the screw of the pin joint covered by the hip plastic.

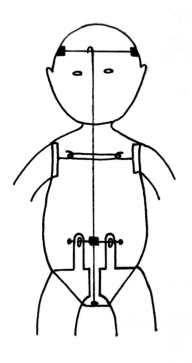

The hidden walking mechanism on the smaller slimmer 'serious'-faced 13" and 16" Roddy walking dolls.

Rosebud Dolls Ltd/ Nene Plastics Ltd

1947 TO 1967

Taking over his father's business in 1934, which had been making a range of wooden toys, dolls' houses, rocking horses, forts and farms etc, Mr Eric T. Smith started manufacturing composition dolls in 1947, registering the trademark 'Rosebud' in that year. The composition dolls were made in several small sizes, 6" to 17", with both painted and sleeping eyes, moulded hair and wigs, and a mouth said to resemble a rosebud, hence the trademark. One of the original moulds was later used by Roddy for hard plastic dolls. By 1950 the company was making hard plastic dolls from several face moulds, the first of which were the babies and girls in 6" and 7" sizes called **Rosebud Miniatures**. The 6" babies had curved arms with a clenched fist and a thumb it could 'suck'. These little babies were made with moulded hair for boys or wigs for girls, jointed limbs, sleeping painted eyes and

Maker: Rosebud Dolls
Doll name: **Miniatures**
Size: 7"/18cm
Marks: none
Date: late 1940s

Composition forerunner of the hard plastic miniatures, with painted eyes and features and glued-on mohair wig.
(Collection Denise and Tony Slade)

Maker: Rosebud Dolls
Doll name: unknown
Size: 11½"/21cm
Marks: 'Rosebud Made in England'
Date: late 1940s

A composition doll with moulded hair, painted eyes, jointed limbs and a rosebud mouth.
(Collection Christine Wimsey)

Maker: Rosebud Dolls
Doll name: none
Size: 17"/44cm
Marks: 'Rosebud Made in England'
Date: late 1940s

Composition doll with sleeping eyes, mohair wig and rosebud mouth.
(Collection Christine Wimsey)

Maker: Rosebud Dolls Ltd/Nene Plastics Ltd
Doll name: none
Sizes: 10"/25.5cm, 13"/33cm, 13"/33cm
Marks: 'Rosebud Made in England'
Dates: 1953, 1950s, 1955

Two unusual Rosebud girls, both of which
were available in pink and black hard plastic.
The baby was a popular model and sold
throughout the 50s. It was also available in
chocolate brown and black in all sizes.

Maker: Rosebud Dolls
Doll name: **Miniatures**
Size: 7"/18cm
Marks: 'Made in England'
Date: late 1947

Three composition miniatures, two with brunette and auburn wigs and on the right a black model with moulded head. All three have painted eyes and features. The centre doll has silver shoes and would probably have been originally dressed as a fairy.

no lashes, in white and black plastic, dressed or undressed. They came presentation boxed in little straw Moses baskets trimmed with organdie. The 7" little girls had a 'sucked-in cheeks' expression and came with the same moulded hair for boys or wigs for girls, with straight legs, jointed arms and sleeping painted eyes. Black dolls also came in a variety of costumes including fairies, brides, sailors, national costume, Scottish, story-book characters and naked for dressing at home. A 7" **Upside Down Doll** had a white head one end and a black head the other. It is unlikely the doll was in full production as it is very rare.

Many knitting patterns for lovely little clothes were printed in women's magazines (especially *Women's Weekly*) throughout the Fifties for this sweet little girl doll, and the babies. Late Fifties miniatures had glassene-type sleeping eyes replacing the earlier painted sleeping eyes. Rosebud dolls also produced a 7" **Costume Doll Series** of slimmer dolls with mohair wigs in various national costumes. Larger bent-leg babies from 9" to 17" came with an open-closed mouth, teeth and tongue, moulded hair or wigs, voice boxes, sleeping eyes with lashes and dressed in baby-style outfits with bonnet, or, naked to be dressed at home. Black dolls also came in this range, with curly astrakhan wigs, hula-hula grass skirts and bead necklaces.

Rosebud girl dolls were very attractive and came in the same sizes, 11" to 16" tall, some with voice boxes. They had the typical Rosebud mouth and were straight legged and fully jointed, with sleeping eyes,

Maker: Rosebud
Doll name: unknown toddler
Size: 11"/28cm
Marks: 'Rosebud Made in England' in signature form across back
Date: 1952

A beautiful little toddler with an old-fashioned curled wig, sleeping eyes, rosy cheeks, open-closed mouth, two teeth and tongue. She wears a Rosebud print dress trimmed with lace.

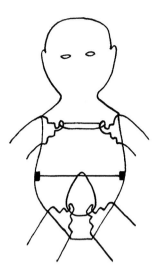

Diagram of elastic stringing on the 6"/15cm Thumbsuck Babies. The head is fixed and the legs are strung from a bar across the waist. The arms are strung independently.

ABOVE RIGHT
Maker: Rosebud Dolls
Doll name: **Thumbsuck Babies**
Size: 6"/15cm
Marks: 'Rosebud Made in England'
Date: 1950s

On the right a 1952 baby with blonde astrakhan wig, sleeping eyes without lashes, one-piece body with strung arms and legs. On the left a late 1950s boy with moulded head, sleeping eyes without lashes, one-piece body with strung arms and legs.

CENTRE RIGHT
Three early babies with painted eyes. The marks on these early dolls were in capitals. The signature form trademark came at the end of the '50s.
(Collection Denise and Tony Slade)

RIGHT
Maker: Rosebud Dolls
Doll name: **Thumbsuck Babies**
Size: 6"/15cm
Marks: 'Rosebud Made in England'
Date: late 1950s

Three black babies with glassene eyes. Markings in signature form. Doll on right has astrakhan wig and 'grass' skirt.

LEFT
Maker: Rosebud Dolls
Doll name: **Thumbsuck Babies**
Size: 6"/15cm
Marks: 'Rosebud Made in England'
Date: 1950s

On the left a late 1950s boy with moulded head.
On the right a black 1952 baby with black astrakhan wig, sleeping eyes without lashes, one-piece body with strung arms and legs.

Maker: Rosebud Dolls
Doll name: **Thumbsuck Babies**
Size: 6"/15cm
Marks: 'Rosebud Made in England'
Date: early 1950s, late 1950s, early 1960s

Three moulded-hair babies in original packing showing early 1950s box with painted eye doll; late 1950s cellophane bag with glassene eye doll; early 1960s cellophane bag with glassene eye doll and header card with 1960s logo. Notice how the colour of the dolls gets progressively pinker! (Collection Denise and Tony Slade)

ABOVE RIGHT
Naked 6"/15cm Rosebud baby showing fixed head and strung limbs. Notice the bent arm enabling the baby to 'suck' its thumb.

RIGHT
Doll mark on 6"/15cm Rosebud Thumbsuck Baby: 'Rosebud Made in England'.

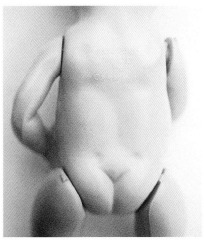

ABOVE LEFT
Maker: Rosebud Dolls
Doll name: **Miniatures**
Size: 7"/18cm
Marks: 'Rosebud Made in England'
Date: 1950

A moulded-hair boy on the left and an auburn-wigged girl on the right. Both dolls have sleeping eyes without lashes, straight legs and jointed arms. These dolls were also made in black versions.

ABOVE RIGHT
Maker: Rosebud Dolls
Doll name: **Miniatures**
Size: 7"/18cm
Marks: 'Rosebud Made in England'
Date: 1950

On the left a blonde-wigged girl and on the right a brunette-wigged girl. Both dolls have sleeping eyes with no lashes, straight legs and jointed arms.

LEFT
Maker: Rosebud Dolls
Doll name: **Miniatures**
Size: 7"/18cm
Marks: 'Rosebud Made in England'
Date: 1960s and 1950s

On the left a black-wigged 1960s girl with glassene eyes and on the right a black-wigged girl from the 1950s with painted eyes.

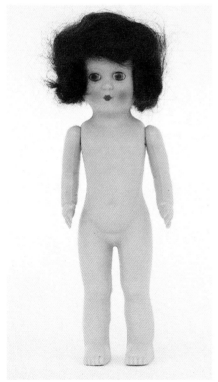

ABOVE
Maker: Rosebud Dolls
Doll name: **Miniatures**
Size: 7"/18cm
Marks: 'Rosebud Made in England'
Date: early 1950s

Four dolls showing wigged and moulded hair, all with painted eyes, standing next to an original box.
(Collection Denise and Tony Slade)

FAR LEFT
Naked body of the 7"/18cm Rosebud Miniature girl. She has a rosy 'sucked-in cheeks' expression, one-piece straight-leg body and jointed arms.

LEFT
This illustration shows the doll mark on the 7"/18cm Miniature boys and girls: 'Rosebud Made in England Patents Pending'.

Maker: Rosebud Dolls
Doll name: **Baby Dolls**
Size: 9¼"/24cm
Marks: 'Rosebud Made in England'
Date: 1950 and throughout the 1950s

Four babies spanning ten years. These dolls were remodelled periodically throughout the 1950s. On the left a 1950 model marked 'Rosebud Made in England Patents Pending' with weighted swinging eyes and no lashes. By the early 1950s they had metal-lidded eyes with eyelashes and were marked 'Rosebud Made in England Pat No 667906'. The mid-1950s issue had sleeping eyes with lashes and an open-closed mouth with tiny tongue but no teeth. Late 1950s dolls were dainty with plastic solid lashes and marked 'Rosebud Made in England'.

Knitting patterns appeared in women's magazines for all four of these different models throughout the decade.

Maker: Rosebud Dolls
Doll name: **Baby Dolls**
Size: 11"/28cm
Marks: 'Rosebud Made in England'
Date: mid-1950s

Moulded hair baby with open-closed mouth with teeth, sleeping eyes and a jointed bent-limb body. These dolls were made in 11", 13", 15" and 17" sizes.

Maker: Rosebud Dolls
Doll name: **Baby Dolls**
Size: 13"/33cm
Marks: 'Rosebud Made in England'
Date: mid-1950s

Black moulded-hair baby with open-closed mouth with teeth, amber sleeping eyes and a jointed bent-limb body.

Maker: Rosebud Dolls
Doll name: none
Size: 15"/38cm
Marks: 'Rosebud Made in England'
Date: 1950s

A black bent-limb baby with open mouth and two teeth.
(Collection Denise and Tony Slade)

. Maker: Rosebud Dolls
Doll name: **Baby Dolls**
Size: 11"/28cm
Marks: 'Rosebud' on back of neck, 'Made in England' across shoulders
Date: mid-1950s

An unusual closed lips baby with moulded hair, sleeping eyes and jointed bent-limb body.

ABOVE LEFT
Maker: Rosebud Dolls
Doll name: **Baby Dolls**
Size: 17"/43cm
Marks: 'Rosebud Made in England'
Date: early 1950s

The largest of the bent-limb baby dolls with moulded hair, sleeping eyes and jointed limbs, pictured in her original box as she was sold.

ABOVE RIGHT
Maker: Rosebud
Doll name: **Baby Dolls**
Size: 17"/43cm; 11"/28cm; 15"/38cm
Marks: All: 'Rosebud Made in England' in signature form across shoulders
Date: early- to mid-1950s

A group of three different sizes of Rosebud babies. The 17" pale baby on the left has sleeping blue eyes, moulded hair and a ma-ma voice box with grille in her back. She is wearing a Swiss broderie anglais dress. The 11" baby in the centre has sleeping amber eyes, voice box with grille in her back and a curly astrakhan wig. She wears a pink rosebud print dress. The baby on the right has moulded hair, amber eyes, voice box with grille in her back and wears a pink organdie nightie. All three babies have open-closed mouths with tongue and teeth.

SIRDAR

c5436
14/16" Dolls

3ply

This knitting pattern was available in the early 1960s for the Rosebud baby.

She'd love a Rosebud doll

ABOVE RIGHT

Maker: Rosebud Dolls
Doll name: **Baby Dolls**
Size: 9"/23cm
Marks: 'Rosebud Made in England'
Date: 1950s

Two different black Rosebud babies with sleeping eyes and fully-jointed limbs, sitting next to an original box.

RIGHT

Maker: Rosebud Dolls
Doll name: none
Sizes: 13"/33cm, 11"/28cm
Marks: 'Rosebud Made in England'
Date: early 1950s

On the left an unusual early baby. On the right a black baby with closed mouth. (Collection Denise and Tony Slade)

LEFT AND BELOW LEFT
Maker: Rosebud Dolls
Doll name: none
Sizes: 9"/23cm
Date: early 1960s

Two boxed babies with additional outfits and shoes. On the left with hat rack, and on the right with drawer space.
(Collection Denise and Tony Slade)

Rosebud baby doll showing signature doll mark found on all 1950s baby dolls.

ABOVE LEFT
Maker: Rosebud Dolls
Doll name: **Girl Dolls**
Size: 13"/33cm
Marks: 'Rosebud' on back of neck, 'Made in England' across shoulders
Date: mid-1950s

Closed lips girl doll with brunette mohair wig, sleeping eyes and elastic-strung jointed body. This model was also made as a knee-joint doll.

CENTRE
Maker: Rosebud Dolls
Doll name: **Girl Dolls**
Size: 13"/33cm
Marks: 'Rosebud' on back of neck, ''Made in England' across shoulders

A black, closed-lips girl doll with black mohair wig, sleeping amber eyes and an elastic-strung jointed body. This model was also made as a knee-joint doll.

ABOVE RIGHT
Maker: Rosebud Dolls
Doll name: none
Size: 17"/43cm
Marks: 'Rosebud Made in England'
Date: 1950s

Open-closed mouth with teeth, sleeping eyes and the remnants of a once plaited wig, long since chopped off.

FAR LEFT
Maker: Rosebud Dolls
Doll name: none
Size: 11"/28cm
Marks: 'Rosebud Made in England'
Date: 1950s

Black girl with open-closed mouth and teeth, black saran wig, jointed limbs.
(Collection Denise and Tony Slade)

LEFT
Close-up of the Rosebud girl doll on the left. These dolls were also sold naked, to be dressed at home.

and wigs in three colours: blonde, auburn or brunette, in short curly styles, or pigtails (two plaits). Black girls were also made with astrakhan, short curly or longer two-plait black wigs. The dolls wore stylish dresses, skirts and tops or sunsuits in cotton fabrics. Hand-assisted walkie girls were also made in the above sizes and styles, some with voice boxes. **Knee-Joint Walking Dolls** were also available in the 13" and 17" girl doll sizes. These were walking jointed dolls and could kneel, walk and sit very realistically. They had sleeping eyes and a blonde, auburn or brunette wig, with a black wig on the black doll.

Miss Rosebud was another very popular line, nearly 8" tall and fully jointed. She had a very pretty rosy-cheeked face, sleeping eyes and a variety of wigs in five colours: pale blonde, fair, auburn, brown and black, in many different styles. She was exquisitely dressed in dozens of different styles, including national costumes, fairy stories, sports outfits, play clothes and day dresses etc. She was marked 'Miss Rosebud Made in England' on her back. The doll was discontinued in 1958 when the moulds were sold to the Amanda Jane, Roddy and Faerie Glen companies. In 1952 the Rosebud little booklet showed another sweet doll called a **Hair-Do Doll**; nearly 15" tall, she had a wig that could be shampooed and set, and came boxed complete with comb, curlers and shampoo. She had a ma-ma voice box and was dressed in a pink camiknicker. Suffice it to say, if the doll's wig was shampooed, brushed and set, too often it did eventually disintegrate!

◀ **PAGE 124 LEFT**
Maker: Rosebud Dolls
Doll name: none
Size: 15"/38cm
Marks: 'Rosebud Made in England'
Date: 1950s

Black and white girls with sleeping eyes, open-closed mouths with two teeth. Fully jointed with saran wigs.
(Collection Denise and Tony Slade)

FAR LEFT
Maker: Rosebud Dolls
Doll name: **Knee Joint Dolls**
Size: 17"/43cm
Marks: 'Rosebud' on back of neck, 'Made in England' across shoulders
Date: mid-1950s

Lovely black walking knee joint doll with black mohair wig, sleeping eyes, closed lips and elastic-jointed arms and knees.

LEFT
Maker: Rosebud
Doll name: **Knee Joint Doll**
Size: 17"/43cm
Marks: 'Made in England' across back
Date: 1955

This has a brown mohair wig, sleeping eyes and rosebud mouth. Her head turns when she is walked along and her arms and knees are elastic strung. She wears a replica of her original dress.

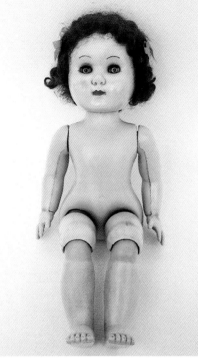

Maker: Rosebud
Doll name: **Walkie Talkie**
Size: 13"/33cm
Marks: 'Rosebud' on back of neck
Date: 1955

An attractive little girl with open-closed mouth, gauze tongue and two teeth, sleeping eyes and grille in stomach. Fair mohair wig which has been trimmed. Head moves as she is walked along.

Maker: Rosebud
Doll name: **Knee Joint Doll**
Size: 17"/43cm
Marks: 'Rosebud' on back of neck, 'Made in England' across shoulders
Date: 1957

This doll has an identical body to the one on page 120, but with a vinyl head with rooted short hair and a different face with sleeping blue eyes.

Naked plastic body of knee joint doll. She has a conventional walking mechanism and elastic-strung arms and knees.

◀ PAGE 126
Maker: Rosebud
Dolls' names: **Knee Joint Dolls**
Sizes: 17"/43cm; baby 6"/15cm
Marks: 'Made in England' across back
Date: 1955

Dolls' tea party with two Rosebud knee joint girls sitting naturally at the table. On the left with auburn mohair wig, sleeping blue eyes and a tiny Kleeware thumbsuck in the pocket of her teddy print dress. On the right a black knee joint girl with black mohair wig, amber sleeping eyes and a pretty turquoise print dress. On the table a Chad Valley aluminium tea set from 1949 and on the floor, her dolly is a tiny Rosebud baby with moulded hair and sleeping eyes.

Shown naked, the Miss Rosebud doll has strung head and limbs, mohair wig, sleeping eyes without lashes, closed lips, and measures 7¹/₂"/19cm tall.

Maker: Rosebud Dolls
Doll name: **Miss Rosebud**
Size: 7¹/₂"/19cm
Marks: 'Miss Rosebud Made in England'
Date: 1952

Three Miss Rosebud dolls showing auburn wig on the left, blonde wig in the centre and brunette wig on the right. All the dolls have sleeping eyes without lashes, closed lips and fully-jointed chubby bodies.

Maker: Rosebud Dolls
Doll name: **Miss Rosebud**
Size: 7¹/₂"/19cm
Marks: 'Miss Rosebud Made in England'
Date: 1958

Undressed Miss Rosebud sitting on her original box.
(Collection Denise and Tony Slade)

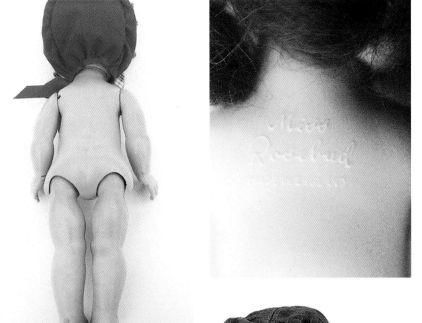

FAR LEFT
FAR LEFT
Rosebud dolls have wonderfully smooth 'seats'. If a Rosebud-type doll is found with only 'Made in England' across the shoulders, a good tip is to compare it with another make and you will soon recognise the smoothness of the Rosebud 'seat'. It is distinguishable from other dolls. Many girl dolls like the one illustrated were marked very faintly 'ROSEBUD' in tiny capitals on the back of the neck, and sometimes 'Made in England' across the shoulders.

LEFT
This illustration shows the doll mark on Miss Rosebud in signature style plus 'Made in England'.

Maker: Rosebud Dolls
Doll name: **Hair-do Doll**
Size: 14¼"/36cm
Marks: 'Rosebud Made in England'
Date: 1952

A Hair-do Doll wearing a pink camiknicker. She came boxed with a doll's hairdressing set to enable the child to practise hairdressing skills. She was a jointed straight-leg doll with mohair wig, sleeping eyes and open-closed mouth with teeth.
(Collection Christine Wimsey)

Pages from a 1952 Rosebud dolls booklet showing **Miss Rosebud** and the **Hair-do Doll**.

More pages from a 1952 Rosebud dolls booklet showing black dolls, **Miniatures**, baby and girl dolls.

Through the Fifties, Rosebud dolls were usually marked with 'Rosebud' in signature form or capitals and 'Made in England' across their backs and sometimes on the back of the head too.

By 1955 Rosebud was experimenting with vinyl, like most of their competitors of the day, and issued several dolls with hard plastic bodies and vinyl, rooted heads, including the **Knee Joint Doll** with a different 'vinyl' face and rooted short hair. The body, though, was identical to the hard plastic versions. Many hard plastic dolls were still being made, of course, as the switch to vinyl was gradual over a couple of years. Rosebud teenage dolls, introduced in 1958, had hard plastic slimmer bodies, an older vinyl face and various rooted hair styles, sleeping eyes, voice box and measured 20" tall. In 1959 a **Miss Rosebud** bride was introduced. She was an updated vinyl doll now in a 14" size with rooted hair and wore a lovely bridal outfit.

By 1960 **Miss Rosebud** had moved to a new factory in Wellingborough and was doubling its previous output of dolls. It introduced a new trademark that year which was a key shape with the 'R' of Rosebud intertwined with a rose and leaf. All dolls after 1960 were marked with the new logo which included an update of the little 7" girl/boy miniature dolls still being presented in hard plastic, but with a new rounder face and glassene sleeping eyes, in both white and black versions, with or without wigs. Also the 6" 'thumbsuck baby' in white and black flesh, now only with moulded hair, glassene sleeping eyes and re-introduced in an early Sixties' catalogue as 'something old something new'. An advertisement in 1961 described the new factory at Wellingborough as 'completely modernised and equipped with the latest up-to-date machinery for making the famous Rosebud dolls and toys, hundreds of girls are now employed by us and the company's own vans will deliver within a two-hundred-mile radius'. A far cry from the small band of workers originally employed by the company in 1947.

During the early Sixties, Rosebud continued to produce a lovely range of baby, toddler, girl dolls in vinyl including more updated **Miss Rosebuds**, now a teenage doll in 15" and 20" sizes, and '**Big Dolls** – child sized dolls as large as life' and almost as real, from 25" to 35" tall. The latter could wear a real baby dress and three-year-old child's clothes.

From this time, Rosebud Dolls were equipped with Mattel talking units as Mattel Inc began amalgamating with Rosebud by the mid-Sixties, introducing many new talking dolls to the Rosebud vinyl range. Mattel finally took control of Rosebud in 1967 and a few of the original Rosebud staff formed their own company, making Blossom Dolls and Toys in vinyl, as the name Rosebud was now owned by Mattel, but during 1970 the name Rosebud was dropped from Mattel's logo.

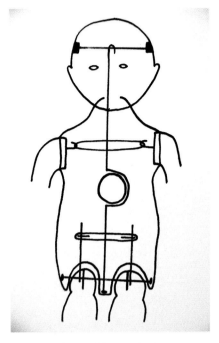

Diagram of the walking mechanism on Rosebud walking dolls. The screw heads on the pin joint are concealed by plastic at the hips. The circle in the centre is the voice box.

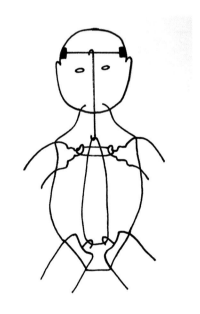

Rough sketch of the stringing on the Rosebud babies during the 1950s. The legs have metal hooks and the arms moulded plastic hooks.

Maker: Rosebud Dolls
Doll name: **Miniatures**
Size: 7"/18cm
Marks: 'Rosebud' in logo form and 'Made in England'
Date: 1960s

Three 1960s Rosebud Miniature girl dolls with auburn, blonde and brunette wigs. All have sleeping eyes without lashes, one-piece straight-leg bodies with jointed arms. Black dolls were also made in this model and without wigs.

Naked 1960s Rosebud **Miniature** 7"/18cm girl doll showing sleeping eyes with no lashes, straight legs and jointed arms.

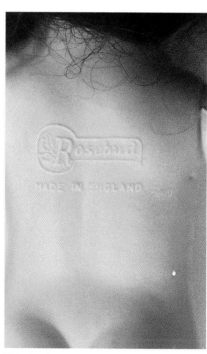

This detail shows the new 1960 logo used on Rosebud dolls from this date, and is pictured on a 7"/18cm **Miniature** girl doll.

Maker: Rosebud Dolls
Doll name: **Teenage Doll**
Size: 20"/51cm
Marks: 'Rosebud Made in England'
Date: 1959

One of the first vinyl Rosebud dolls. The body is hard plastic and the head vinyl with rooted auburn hair. She has an older 'teenage' face and amber sleeping eyes, with a pull-cord talking mechanism and grille in her stomach.

Maker: Rosebud Dolls
Doll name: **Walking Talking Doll**
Size: 24"/61cm
Marks: 'Made in England' across back, 'Rosebud' on back of neck
Date: 1960

Another early vinyl Rosebud with a hard plastic body and vinyl rooted head with hair of soft saran nylon. She is a walking-talking doll with sleeping eyes and carries a small golden bear with a Rosebud label.

Maker: Sarold Manufacturing Co Ltd
Doll name: **Girls and Babies**
Sizes: 7"/18cm, 10"/25.5cm, 3"/7.5cm
Marks: 'Sarold Made in England'
Date: early 1950s

Sarold dolls were made of a very light-weight hard plastic in many sizes from 3" to 25". Many have not survived a child's rough handling and certain sizes are quite difficult to find.

Sarold Manufacturing Co Ltd

1950 THROUGH THE FIFTIES

The first thing that I and many other collectors remember of Sarold dolls is that they were sold from the sectioned counter displays in Woolworths stores throughout Britain from 1950 onwards. Each counter section had a different size and therefore different price tag on many small, naked dolls. The larger dolls were boxed and displayed on the upright shelves.

The Sarold Manufacturing Company Limited, to give the firm its full title, had an office and factory at Kirkby, Liverpool, during the Fifties and an address in London for distribution. They made injection-moulded cellulose acetate (hard plastic) dolls in large quantities and in sizes ranging from 3" to 25". The Sarold trademark was registered in 1950 and a contract to supply – among the usual outlets – Woolworths stores was signed in the early Fifties.

The dolls, bent-leg babies and toddlers and straight-leg girls, had sleeping eyes, moulded or wigged heads and the most gorgeous old-fashioned chubby faces with rosy cheeks. The 3" baby had sleeping eyes, a one-piece body and push-fit jointed limbs. The larger sizes had elastic-strung heads and limbs, and various styles and colours of wig included the two plaits style on the girls and moulded hair on the babies, with the larger sizes having voice boxes.

The 7" girls had sleeping eyes with no lashes and some had painted-on shoes and socks. They all had jointed elastic-strung limbs with metal hooks. Another range of 7" dolls, with a one-piece body with straight legs and only the arms jointed, sleeping eyes with no lashes, was the Souvenir National Costume dolls. They were dressed as English, Scottish, Welsh and Irish boys and girls with painted-on shoes and socks. They too had the familiar, old-fashioned face and rosy cheeks and were presentation boxed.

The Sarold dolls were reasonably inexpensive and made in the traditional way in fairly thin flesh-coloured plastic with the limbs and bodies seamed together lengthwise down each limb. Black plastic larger dolls were made by this company but in smaller quantities, as were the smaller sizes. All are extremely hard to find today. All the dolls were marked 'Sarold Made in England' across their backs, making them easy to identify.

Maker: Sarold Mfg Co Ltd
Doll name: none
Size: 3"/7.5cm
Marks: 'Sarold Made in England'
Date: early 1950s

A push-fit jointed hard plastic baby with fixed head, sleeping eyes and moulded hair. These tiny babies were sold naked from counter displays in Woolworths stores throughout the early 1950s.

Maker: Sarold
Doll name: unknown
Size: 25"/64cm
Marks: 'Sarold Manufacturing Co Ltd Made in England' centre back
Date: 1950

This large baby has moulded hair, sleeping blue eyes, open mouth with two bottom teeth, ma-ma voice box with grille in her back. She is lightweight but chunky looking with an old-fashioned face. She wears a real baby's clothes. One of the author's childhood toys. This version was also made with straight legs and dressed as a girl with a blonde or brunette wig in tight curls.

Naked body of Sarold 7"/18cm girl showing jointed limbs which were elastic strung.

Maker: Sarold Mfg Co Ltd
Doll name: none
Size: 7"/18cm
Marks: 'Sarold Made in England'
Date: early 1950s

Three Sarold girls with fully-jointed bodies, showing three different wigs, short brunette on the left, blonde plaits centre and brunette plaits on the right. They had sleeping eyes without lashes and painted-on shoes.

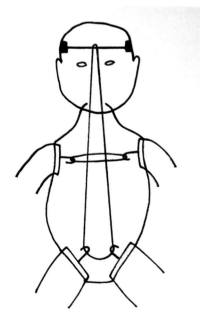

FAR LEFT
Diagram of the 7"/18cm little Sarold girls showing elastic stringing and metal hooks.

LEFT
Doll mark 'Sarold Made in England' as it appears on the backs of the 7"/18cm Sarold girl and all Sarold dolls.

Williams & Steer Manufacturing Co Ltd

1940s AND 1950s

Known for manufacturing hard plastic heads, limbs and accessories for the doll-making industry in the late Forties and early Fifties. This North London-based firm and its sister company S.F. Williams Ltd, manufactured many parts for other doll companies, buyers and traders. Their own small series of dolls was produced from 1948 and included a doll they advertised as **Mignon**, presumably after the small and delicately formed plant with grey-green flowers. If so, her name belies her as she was a large and unusual novelty doll. The doll could be plugged in to any wireless or radio set and the sound would come from the loudspeaker in the doll's body.

Other dolls produced under their own name were small walking boys and girls, rather like the 12" **Roddy** series. They too were 12" tall with a distinctive face which had moulded, painted eyebrows, sleeping eyes and parted red lips. The hands were unusual with individual fingers and thumb and bent elastic-strung arms. The walking mechanism was the traditional rod from crutch to head type, with legs and head moving in unison. These small dolls had wigs for girls and moulded heads for boys, both with moulded-on strap-type shoes. The dolls are usually marked across their backs 'W. & ST Made in England', and were originally boxed with a wrist swing ticket stating 'I can walk, I can sit, I move my head, I can sleep', and on the reverse, 'You can wash, comb and set my hair'. Needless to say, the wigs soon disintegrated if they were washed and combed too frequently. The dolls illustrated have not had their hair washed or dressed. Never having seen baby dolls made by this company, I cannot verify whether bent-limb dolls were made under their own label.

◀ FAR LEFT PAGE 138
Maker: Williams & Steer
Doll name: unknown
Size: 12"/30.5cm
Marks: 'W & ST Made in England'
Date: early 1950s

These walking dolls had distinctive faces and hands with a body that resembled the 12"/30.5cm Roddy girl. They had moulded painted eyebrows, sleeping blue eyes, closed lips, mohair wigs on girls and moulded hair on boys. The shoes were moulded and painted also.

Maker: Williams & Steer Mfg Co Ltd
Doll name: unknown
Size: 12"/30.5cm
Marks: 'W & ST Made in England'
Date: early 1950s

Another 12"/30.5cm walking girl with a blonde mohair wig. She has the same face, body and hands as her brother and sister at left.

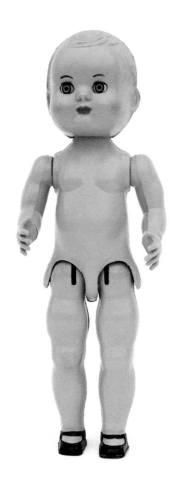

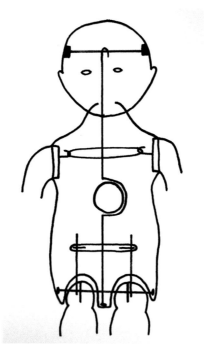

This diagram shows walking mechanism with screw-on pin-joint covered by hip plastic and elastic-jointed arms. The Williams & Steer doll was typical of other walking dolls of this era.

Naked body showing walking legs and jointed arms and head on a Williams & Steer 12"/30.5cm boy.

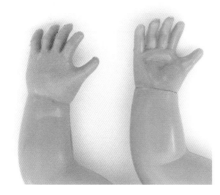

This illustration shows a close-up of the hands with nicely moulded individual fingers.

Close-up of Williams & Steer doll mark showing the initials 'W & St Made in England', which appeared on these attractive dolls.

Maker: Williams & Steer
Doll name: unknown
Size: 12"/30.5cm
Marks: 'W & ST Made in England'
Date: early 1950s

This illustration shows the 12"/30.5cm girl in her original outfit with swing ticket which states, 'I can walk – I can sit – I can sleep – I can move my head'; on the reverse, 'You can wash – comb and set – my hair'. (Collection Christine Wimsey)

Glossary

Anatomical dolls Showing the structure of the anatomy, including sexual organs.

Antique dolls Usually dolls over 100 years old, but often includes dolls over 75 years old.

Celluloid Synthetic material made from camphor, nitrocellulose and alcohol – very inflammable. Made into thin sheets and moulded into heads and/or limbs and bodies.

Composition Mixtures of either shredded paper, sawdust, leather, shavings or wood pulp mixed with sand, plaster resin, pumice powder or flour and fixed with a strong animal glue, moulded to head or body shape, set hard and glazed. Most doll makers used their own secret recipe and therefore 'composition' dolls were made from various ingredients as listed above.

Fixed/stationary Eyes of glass or synthetics stuck into position so that they do not move or the doll does not sleep when laid flat.

Flirting Eyes that move from side to side as well as open and close.

Glassene Eyes of synthetic material made to look like glass, very often stationary.

Hand-assisted walker/talker Doll held by the hand or waist and assisted to walk. Fitted with ma-ma voice box.

Hard plastic Doll made from injection-moulded cellulose acetate.

Jointed limbs Dolls with some movable joints either at head, shoulders, elbows, wrists, waist, hips, knees, ankles. A doll can have as many as fourteen joints or as few as one. On average, a doll has five joints: head, arms and legs, that move.

Ma-ma voice box Small, cylindrical box diaphragm inserted in doll's back or stomach, that makes a noise like ma-ma when doll is tilted backwards and forwards.

Modern or post-war Dolls made after the Second World War, 1945 to the present day.

Moulded Hair shape moulded with head, and painted to give illusion of hair.

Open-closed mouth Parted lips (sometimes showing teeth), but there is no opening. Sometimes a fine white line is painted between the lips, giving the appearance of teeth.

Painted eyes Eye sockets not cut out when moulded, but painted afterwards to look like eyes in a fixed position.

Polythene Thermoplastic material.

Pre-war Dolls made before the Second World War, from 1900 to 1939. There were not so many dolls made during the war years as the factories were needed to make munitions.

PVC Poly-vinyl-chloride.

Rag and soft body Made from fabric or vinyl and stuffed with soft synthetic fibre.

Reproduction Dolls made from a mould taken from an original or old doll.

Rooted hair Nylon or polyester fibre stitched into the head in rows, brushed and trimmed to style.

Rubber Elastic solid made from the milky juice (latex) of certain plants.

Saran Soft nylon hair.

Side-glancing Eyes painted or set so that they are looking to one side rather than forward.

Sleeping Eyes that open and close as the doll is stood upright or laid flat.

Talking/laughing Doll with talking/laughing mechanism in its back, either operated by a pull cord or batteries and tiny pre-recorded discs.

Vinyl Material made from synthetic vinyl compounds, PVC and polythene.

Walking doll Doll that walks a few steps with the aid of batteries inserted into the body mechanism and switched on.

Wig Mohair, nylon, rayon or animal hair glued or rooted into a thin canvas shape and glued to the doll's head.

Index